God's Love beyond Despair and Trauma:
Finding your Divine Purpose

Patricia C.Friend

InfusedMedia Co. LLC
www.infusedmedia.co
1-888-251-6088

INTRODUCTION

I Find myself at times waking up from sleep feeling numb inside knowing that one day I will have to die. Like my suicide attempt I really didn't want to die but it was something I felt like I had to do. I ask myself, why did God save me from myself? Will I see the Rapture of the Church and not have to die? I have to believe that the trials and the trauma in my life were for something good that only God could use as a tool in his hands so that I could one day by his grace, help those who are in great despair feeling all lost and that there isn't any hope. I really believed that at one time and remember telling God that I was living life just burning time until my death. That is a very difficult place to be in while trying to function and live life every day as normal as possible.

I never told anyone about my depression and loss of hope but knew one day I would and wanted God somehow to get glory from my pain inside of me. While living this life of mine in despair I never had any friends who cared much for me unless I was sitting in a therapist office and for me, it's not the same thing.

I always wondered, why be born if life has been the way it has been? I soon began to understand God's love for me and decided one day that just to experience his overwhelming love for me was worth being born and dying for. I also learned that this is something that could never be taken from me like so many other things have by others. This gives me great peace. It is my hope that in these pages will be strong evidence that the Bible and Jesus Christ himself is all powerful and able to heal and save under severe trial and trauma. I would have never believed that I would be able to live my life healed and as a whole person after all the things that have happened to me.

If I can become a survivor so can you through Jesus Christ, our Lord. There is power in the blood of the Lamb. I know that everything I have gone through, as bad as it has been, is Father filtered and that God loves me supremely and will never leave me or forsake me. Even at my lowest moment, God has been there for me.

This is something I have been taught by God through my suffering and for that I am grateful and because of my trials and trauma I feel that I am a stronger person when faced with very difficult things. I am a survivor through Jesus Christ my Lord and praise him for the healing that has taken place in my life.

The pain has eased a lot, here is my story:

CHAPTER

1

To start, I was born December 22nd 1964 in Charleston, South Carolina. South Carolina is a beautiful place and there are rivers that are all around Charleston, woods with tall trees and creeks that we used to swim in as children. When my Mom and Dad were married life seemed to be wonderful. My Dad seemed to be a very happy man and had what I would call a good marriage to my Mother.

I have a brother and sister who are younger than I am. Leslie is two years younger than I am and my brother, Jim is five years younger than me. At Christmas time my Dad would shower us kids with many gifts. We loved Christmas mornings and had a lot of toys to play with. I will always remember those days and how content and loved I felt as a child. Time goes so fast and it would have been nice to live in those days forever.

My parents were divorced when I was 8 years old. It didn't affect me as bad as it did my sister. My brother was too young to remember my parent's divorce. The day that my Dad packed and was leaving us, my sister ran down the drive way at our home, begging my Dad to take her with him. Leslie was devastated at 6 years old.

I on the other hand I handled my parent's divorce a little differently. I laid in bed the night my Dad left us and in my mind tore my heart in half and gave part of my heart to my Mother and the other part of my heart to my Dad. That was the only way at my age to deal with the situation I felt.

At twenty-eight my Mom was alone and forced to take a job as a secretary. She had taken typing in high school and got the job she applied for. We kids were with baby sitters some of the time and then eventually, we began to take care of ourselves while my mother worked.

In the summers we kids would have a blast. We would ride bikes with two neighbor boys at about our age. The youngest boy 8, he was my age, and the oldest 10 years old. We loved to go swimming and in the marshes near the rivers, we would go crawling and sliding around in the mud. We were not aware of all of the alligators that were probably all around us. We just wanted to have fun and we did.

I remember one afternoon I decided to go swimming alone so I got on my bike and peddled down to the river where a dock was. I put my bike on a path near the dock and it was obvious that my bike belonged to a little girl. I had a basket with a pattern of flowers on the handle bars that I would carry things in.

As I was swimming I heard a car pull up. The car had what we called in that day, hippies that were partying and one of the guys got out of the car and ran onto the dock. As a child I felt like God had told me to swim under the dock, grab the poles that were supporting the dock and be quiet. I felt as though I was in danger. The hippie guy looked around for a few minutes and then ran back to the car and drove away.

I knew at that moment that God had protected me and after a few minutes I got on my bike and peddled as fast as I could to get home. I never went swimming alone again and it took some time for me to settle down. I was really afraid.

I had really bad asthma when I was a child and I remember my Mom going to work as I lay in bed gasping for air. I thought I was going to die. My sister and brother were at school on these days and I was home alone. I would call my Mom at work and tell her that I couldn't breathe and she would just tell me to lay down in bed until she got home.

After about three or four days of gasping for air, my Mom would take me to the doctor and he would give me a shot and once again I could breathe again. It was horrible when I had asthma attacks. I learned that I couldn't do a lot of running with the other kids at school. I would bring notes to school from my Mom to keep me from having to run in physical education class.

My Dad would come to the house and pick up us kids to go out with him every two weeks on Saturdays. We would go to the movies, skating and swimming. Once in a while we would go to our Grandmother's house and visit with her. My Grandmother, we called Yia-Yia. My Yia-Yia was my dad's mother. She was Greek and very strict with us kids.

I didn't understand for years why my Mom and Dad got a divorce but later on as I grew older, my Yia-Yia told me the reason. Yia-Yia said my parents got divorced because my Mom would always go out on the weekends and leave us kids at home with my Dad. Mom began drinking and would party with new friends that she had met at the places she would go to. My Dad had finally had enough and divorced her.

I loved my Mom and hated to see her go through all the things she had gone through while I was growing up. Her life tragically ended in a car accident when she was 42 years old, I was 22. I believe my Mom just got caught up in the wrong relationships with people. She was an alcoholic and tried many times to get help. She would go to detox in hospitals and get the help she needed but she just could not stay sober very long.

Alcohol eventually took her life and I know my Mom didn't mean for this to happen. I'll forever miss my Mom, but made a recent promise to myself that I would do everything in my life now to try and give her life meaning and purpose through the things that I do in mine. I certainly don't think that my Mom would have wanted me to try and commit suicide later on in my life. I believe at the end of my Mom's life all she had was God's grace for her. And I believe that was enough and all that was needed. I learned that God loves my Mom more than I do and that gives me great comfort.

CHAPTER

2

I remember one morning about 2am, I woke up to my Mom's voice yelling at someone and I could hear a man's voice screaming back at her. I was ten years old at this time and the fighting between my Mom and this man scared me. I didn't know what in the world was going on.

The screaming got louder and we kids were really afraid. My Mom had two friends at the house with her that night, Sherry and her boyfriend Clifford. Sherry was thirty years old and Clifford was thirty-one. While the screaming and yelling continued, Sherry and Clifford came into me and my sister's room and put a blanket on the floor and made us kids lay on the blanket. Clifford pulled a gun,a pistol out of his belt and held on to it while we wondered if he was going to shoot someone.

When we asked what was going on, Clifford said that if anything more would have happed he had his gun and we shouldn't worry and he told us to go back to sleep. I could not sleep being so afraid. I wondered if the man that was yelling at my Mom would kill her.

Finally, the screaming and yelling stopped and the man that was yelling back and forth with my Mom finally left the house. Sherry and Clifford went into the kitchen to see if my Mom was okay. Later they left the house too.

I found out later on that Clifford had shot his roommate and he went to prison for murder. I felt, even as a child that Clifford would shoot someone because when he was around he waved his pistol at everyone showing off. He would get drunk when he was at our house with his girlfriend, Sherry and run his mouth a lot. I hated it when they would come to the house. I would go into my room and disappear.

Not long after the night this man was yelling at my Mom, I met him. I got up out of bed about four thirty in the morning. It was a cold morning and I noticed that our front door was opened. With all of my Mother's partying, it didn't surprise me at all. I figured one of her friend's left the door opened so I walked into the living room and closed the door.

I heard my mom knocking on the door, telling me to open the door. I had locked it when I closed it. I opened the front door and when I did, there was a man standing outside talking to my mother. I looked at him and noticed that he was kind of short. He had a lot of muscles and curly brown hair. His hair didn't look like it had been brushed in quite some time and I was a little scared. He was twenty-six and just got back home from Viet Nam.

My mom introduced me as her older child, Christy and asked me to say hello to him. He told my mom it was really cold and asked her if he could come inside. My mom told him if he would go get her children something to eat that she would let him in the house.

My mom asked me if I wanted to go to a convenient store with him and I said I would go. He and I walked over to his Volkswagen car and got in. I wondered if he had been drinking but I didn't ask him about it.

He asked me my age and I told him I was ten years old. We pulled up at the store and they were opened for twenty-four hours. We walked in and my mom's friend asked if baloney sandwiches were alright. I said yes.

He drove us back to the house and my mom let him in. We walked into the house and made sandwiches for him and myself. As I ate I wondered what in the world was this man doing with my mother. I figured this was a new boy-friend of hers and that they were dating.

My mom went out a lot on the weekends and I thought that this guy is who she went out to see.

After I ate my sandwich, I went back to bed for a while and left them in the kitchen talking.

As time went on, about a year later my mom's boy-friend moved in with us. It was a disaster. Every weekend he and my mother would get a baby sitter for us kids and go out drinking together.

When they would get home, he and my mom would yell and scream at one another and throw things. He eventually began hitting my mother and would beat her pretty bad. One night I got into the middle of their fighting and this guy chocked me while my mom watched. My sister Leslie said to him that she was going to call my dad and he told her to go ahead and call.

My sister called dad and told him that this guy chocked me and my dad asked to speak to me. My dad asked me if I was alright and I said I was, then my dad told me to give my mom's boyfriend the phone. I don't know what my dad said to him but by the look on this guy's face made me think that my dad threatened him.

My brother, Jim was asleep during the fighting and I'm glad he was. He was only five years old and would have been really afraid. My brother liked my mom's boy-friend and would not have understood a whole lot of what was happening.

My sister and I went back to bed and listened to the fighting once again. It was a long night and I couldn't wait for it all to end.

The next morning, nothing was said about what had happened that night. Everyone acted as if had never happened and this is what we did every weekend to keep some peace in the family. My mom's boy-friend would often in the mornings, ask my mom what happened to her face and she would tell him that he had hit her that night. He didn't remember a lot of what he had done because he would be in an alcoholic black out. We children remembered and we would never forget it.

It was a horrible thing that was happening and we were powerless over the situation. What does a kid do under these circumstances? We just learned to live with it and function the best we could. My mom and her boy-friend eventually married and we were devastated.

My mom at times in the summer would take us kids to the bars with her on the beach. My step dad would be out with his buddies fishing so my mom would party with her friends. They, at that time, would let us kids into the bars with our parents. I learned to play pool really well. The guys at the bars would let my brother and I play with them. I also would play the pin ball machines in these bars. There was one particular bar on the beach that my mother liked and we would go there a lot. It was called Little Eddie's Bar and the owner was an old man named Eddie. He was a nice man and I liked him a lot. The bar had a lot of customers in the afternoons and evening on the weekends and everyone there seemed to know one another pretty well.

I would go outside the bar onto the beach and sit in the sand, watching my brother, Jim play in the sand and I would listen to the music that was being played on the record box in the bar. Eddie the owner of the bar had large speakers for the music out on a patio deck in the back of the bar. People would come out and sit in the sun having their alcohol until everyone was good and drunk. I always thought that if the people knew how ridiculous they looked and sounded when they talked, they wouldn't drink so much. For them life was a big party.

When I was twelve years old, the owner of the bar, Eddie died. It was a time in my life that I started to think about God. Who he is and how big he is. I remember looking out at the ocean one day when mom took us kids to the bar and thinking to myself that God made this big ocean and my mind began to wonder. That day I felt very close to God and had a feeling of contentment. I knew that God had something I needed and that I needed him. I didn't really know what God had that I needed but I just knew I did want what he had for me.

The part that I always hated about going to Little Eddie's Bar was when it was time to leave. My mom would put us in the car while she was drunk and I remember trying to brace myself in my seat while my mom was swerving off the road and almost crashing into the trees. It was very freighting and my heart would sink down into my stomach. I would ask myself why do we kids have to live like this? It just wasn't fair at all to us. Wondering if we would make it home alive and then have my step dad come home and beat my mom keeping the whole house awake at two and three o'clock in the morning. I began suffering with really bad depression.

I told myself at a young age that my mother would die one-day drinking and driving, so when it did happen, I was already prepared for it. It was really hard living with this fear and my sister, Leslie and I would often call emergency rooms in the morning hours to see if my mom and my step dad where admitted because of a possible car accident.

This is how we kids lived our lives every weekend. It was hard and we even began having to feed ourselves not knowing where our next meal would come from. My mom and step dad would drink my father's child support away. They would use that money in bars and on alcohol.

Eventually, we would be without any supervision at all and we were considered, latch key children. We had a house key and came and went as we pleased. As I grew, I would party on my own. My friends got the alcohol and the smokes and we would all sit at the house and have a good time. I began to really like being on my own. I felt like I had it made. I could do anything I wanted and life was one big party. At the time though, where was God? I had forgotten all about him. I was just trying to survive my life. I had a horrible secret that I couldn't share with anyone I thought and my secret was causing me a lot of depression and I would escape this horrible thing that was happening to me with fantasies in order to handle it. Would it be better to die? Sometimes it seemed that way. My depression got worse.

My mom worked during the week as a secretary. While she was at work I would cut school a lot. I was thirteen years old at this time and the school counselors would contact my mom and tell them that I was missing too many days. I was suffering at this time with severe depression and a lot of times I just could not get out of bed. My mom talked to the school and they all decided to put me in a school for the emotionally handicapped. EH School is what it was called.

I met with the EH school director, Vince. I really didn't want to go to this school at first but then I changed my mind. The school was small and it was called, Horizon House. The class rooms had about five students for two teachers. We were monitored very well and the teachers were very kind to us students. They could tell that I was very depressed but I tried to get with the program. I did well in English and Math but the things going on at home were the same and not getting any better. I began cutting school again.

The school counselor at Horizon House, Ginger, contacted my mom and told her that if I missed anymore school that they would take me to court for truancy. My mom tried to warn me and told me to make it to the bus stop on time in the mornings or I would be going in front of a Judge. I would tell my mom that I missed the bus every day and she was at work and could not get me to the bus stop or take me to school. I wanted to stay home and drink, smoke and listen to music.

I missed more school so Horizon House filed papers and I went to court on a Monday morning. I stood before a Judge in the city of Charleston, South Carolina and he didn't ask me why I was missing school, he just told me I was breaking the law. After the Judge read a lot of papers to me, he sentenced me to Juvenile Jail for a two-week period, in Columbia South Carolina. Columbia was several hours away so my parents could not visit me.

After the hearing I was placed in hand cuffs and put in a van with other kids my age. It would be a long drive. I wondered how I would be able to go so long without a cigarette and at thirteen years old I was in a full blown addiction to nicotine. It was a cold day and I couldn't keep very warm. My depression was still very bad but what could I do? I know now that I needed medication but no one at that time ever put their kids on medication.

The van finally pulled up to a fenced in juvenile detention center. They opened the gate to let the van in and we were marched single file into the building. We were told to change our clothes and to get ready to be shown our rooms. We each had a bag with deodorant, tooth brush and tooth paste. I had to find a brush for my hair. The detention center had us girls share a brush.

We were all thirteen, fourteen and fifteen years old. The girls were on one side of the building ward and the boys were on the opposite side. We only sat together with the boys at breakfast, lunch and dinner. I felt very uncomfortable there at first and was a little shy. Some of the girls asked me my name and I told them Christy and said hello to them. Some of the girls and guys were there in jail for horrible crimes. Theft, fighting, probably some even for murder. When asked what I did to get thrown in jail and I told them truancy they just laughed.

I hated taking a shower with all the girls. We were watched while in the shower and I felt so humiliated. I wasn't used to being undressed around a lot of girls and not to mention being watched showering. It was horrible. Thank goodness our toilets were in stalls!

At night, after lights were out and I lay in bed, I thought about all that goes on at home. In a way I guess I was happy not to be at home with everything that would go on at the house. I wondered about my horrible secret. I was safe for now and who could I talk to about it? I just kept it to myself and was so torn up inside. I didn't know why I had to live through the pain. I did a lot of sleeping there in jail. During the day we could go to our rooms and hang around in there if we wanted to. I took every opportunity to sleep. That was my only way of escape from my thoughts and the pressure that I was under.

In jail they wouldn't let us smoke and I was having a hard time with it. I started smoking when I was nine, in the woods with the neighborhood kids and I became addicted to nicotine at a very young age. I even smoked with all of the asthma that I had and that is not good. I just could not wait to get home so I could smoke. I think the nicotine helped me with my anxiety and I felt I needed something. I was forever stealing my mother's cigarettes and she knew it but just left me alone.

After I was in jail for two weeks, a van picked some of us kids up and drove us back to Charleston to go before another Judge. When we got to the court house, we were told to sit in a waiting room until our name was called. When I was called into court, a Judge had me sit down and he went over some papers and read them to me. I wasn't really listening. After he read me the papers, he released me to my mom.

When my mother and I drove home, we didn't really talk to one another, we just looked at the road. I hated to go home and wished I could go to my dad's house but I wanted a cigarette. As soon as we pulled up in the drive way, I went in and waited for my mom to put down her purse. As soon as she did, I got a cigarette and went outside to smoke it. Finally, that good familiar feeling of nicotine rushed to my head and I became a bit dizzy. I finished my cigarette and went into the house. It was cold outside and warm inside. I went to my room and put an album on and lay down. I thought to myself about what it would be like here this weekend?

I'm sure the same thing as every weekend, beatings and a lot of yelling. I thought about my mom and how sad it was that she could not support us kids on her own without my step dads help financially. If she could I'm sure she would have left him by now. It was a sad situation.

On Tuesday morning, the next day, I went back to school at the Horizon House and everyone there seemed to be glad to see me. I made friends with a boy named Brian. Brian was thirteen and a hand full for the school. He always had a bag of pot and was always high. I didn't smoke pot because it made me paranoid. We became really good friends after some time and had a lot in common. We liked the same music and we liked to drink together.

On the weekends, Brian would come to our house and we would party together with my little brother Jim. Brian always teased my brother but Jim just always laughed. Jim seemed to really like Brian and so did I.

One Saturday night, Brian went to a pantry store and got into a verbal fight with two men there. The two men pulled Brian in the woods behind the store and murdered him. The next day, Sunday the news reported it. I was shocked! I couldn't believe that my little buddie had been killed. He was only thirteen and had his whole life ahead of him.

The Horizon House gave out permission slips to ask the parents of the students to allow their children to attend Brian's funeral. Most of the parents allowed their kids to go to the funeral. It was really sad.

The authorities did eventually catch the two men that killed Brian. We heard that they were fighting over a bag of pot.

It took a while for me to get past the shock and then I realized I had to let him go and get on with surviving my life the way it was going. I missed Brian terribly.

There was a teacher at Horizon House that really cared about me and also, she had Brian in her class just before he was killed. Her name was Miss Likes. She had white long hair, tied in a bun and she was about eighty years old. She lost her husband in World War 2 and was all alone. She began talking to me about Jesus Christ and I was very interested. I didn't know a lot about Jesus but I knew there was a Jesus. I didn't understand I could have a relationship with him though. That was the first time anyone had ever talked to me about him.

I really needed Jesus in my life but I didn't think much about it at the time. I wish I could go back in time and had prayed for my mom. I don't think as a kid I ever prayed. I needed God to put this strange puzzle of my life into order. I know now that Jesus has used my hard times for good.

Miss Likes taught English class and I really loved writing small stories. I did really well in her class and her class was the only one I could tolerate. The other classes I felt were really boring and I didn't like the other teachers very much. I would be ready to go to public high school into the tenth grade the following year. The teachers at Horizon House tried to prepare me for this change. I would be sixteen the following year.

I did tell some of the teachers about my mom's drinking but I didn't tell them everything about what went on in our home. I was afraid that they would put us kids in foster homes and that we would be away from our mom.

The thing I learned about my mom's drinking and the way she lived, she was trapped in an addiction that she could not get free from. I learned how strong addiction is, being a smoker on and off for forty years. I'm fifty-three now and have been a smoker since I was nine years old. I have tried everything I can think to quit smoking and I am still trying. I've learned to never give up on things. I hope one day to be free from addiction.

When you need your fix, you don't care how much it costs, what time it is and how inconvenient it is for yourself and others. My mom wanted to stop drinking but she never could. My mom went to Alcoholic meetings and was in recovery hospitals on many occasions.

The problem that I believe she had was that she had to go back to the same environment and the same situation at home. With all of that going on I feel that she didn't have a chance to recover. When I saw her laying in her casket at forty-two years old, I felt that she was resting in God's grace and Jesus love for her. She did call me one day from a detox hospital and told me that she made Jesus her Lord and Savior. I used to worry about her salvation but I have to trust Jesus with that. Tragic things happen to us in our lives but the story isn't over. God is still on the throne and has deep love for everyone. He can make a miracle out of a mess in someone's life.

Never think God is finished with someone. I believe that life doesn't end at death, it only just begins. How I have such hope is truly a gift from the Holy Spirit. God has truly healed me from all and has filled my heart at times with his overflowing love. The Bible says that God is love. I have to admit that God is still teaching me to forgive others. It is a slow process but I'm getting there.

I know to forgive others, helps me. To forgive others does not mean we have to still be in an abusive relationship with these people, it only means that healing takes place inside of our hearts and we're opening the door for God to restore to us what these abusive people have done to us and robbed us from. Sometimes the pain is so deep but it doesn't have to hurt forever. Jesus works miracles.

Joel 2:25

And it shall come to pass that whoever calls on the name of the Lord shall be saved.

I have a great deal of love for my mom. While writing these pages I'm not trying to hurt my mother's reputation in any way. It is my hope that people will understand that these things happen and I want to express how God has enabled me to live through these things. It broke my heart to see my mom live through the things that she did. I hated to see my mom's beatings and verbal abuse every weekend but as a child, there was nothing I could do to make things better for her in this situation. All I can do now is remember the good times I had with my mom and there were some. I miss my mom at times and will never forget her.

Addictions are a horrible thing and breaks up many families. I have seen a lot of people die due to alcohol and drug addiction. It is my hope that people will get free from addiction in their lives. I know I for one, need all the help I can get with smoking. I'm an addict too. I know prayer works and I will keep asking for help in order that I may be free and able to put Jesus first, above all else. I know he is faithful and can help me and others to be victorious in our lives, free from addiction, and healed and whole in our hearts.

CHAPTER

3

Before I write this chapter, I would like to say that I feel a lot of shame and humiliation about the things that have happened to me. I have been slandered about things, gossiped about and laughed at, even by people at church. I now thank God for the slander and gossip because the pain that I have from this has enabled me to write and share about the terrible secret I've had all of my childhood. I also write these things because I have love for God and believe this is what he wants me to do in order to help those who have been through the same things.

Before my mother and father were divorced, when I was really young, about six years old and my sister four years old, my mom would take us to a driving range for golf and the owner was a nice man that we called Uncle Vic. My sister and I would hit golf balls while my mom and Uncle Vic talked inside of the building. Uncle Vic also had goats on his driving range and my sister and I would feed them my mon's cigarettes.

Uncle Vic was about fifty years old at this time and retired early from the military. He was an officer and taught the guys in the marines to shoot guns properly. He seemed very friendly to my sister Leslie, and I and we always got all the soda and chips that we wanted while we were at his driving range. When we would leave, Uncle Vic would hug and kiss us good bye and we really liked him.

Later when we were a few years older, when my mom and dad divorced, Uncle Vic would come by the house to see us and he would sit and talk with my mom. One afternoon he asked me if I wanted to come to his house to play and spend the night. I told my mom that I wanted to go and my mom agreed to allow me to spend the night with him.

We packed my overnight pajamas and a few other things and he and I left the house about three o'clock in the afternoon. We drove to an apartment complex and parked. I didn't know where we were because we children knew that he lived in a home with who we call, Aunt Mookie. I found out that he and my Aunt Mookie were separated and living apart from one another.

A couple of hours after we got to his apartment, he told me it was time for my shower. It was about six pm. I was surprised that he wanted me to take a shower because I didn't always take a shower at night. Mostly in the morning I would bathe. I also didn't get a chance to play any at all and wanted to. My mom also let me stay up a little longer because I was now nine years old and she would allow me to watch television until about eight thirty in the evening.

In the bathroom, Uncle Vic undressed me and I felt very ashamed because I didn't want anyone to see me undressed especially him. He then undressed himself and got in the shower with me. I had never seen a man undressed and was very afraid. I didn't know what to do and I knew that what I was going through was not normal. It just didn't feel right to me.

I felt in the back of my head his erection and I was really afraid. I felt very violated but being a child what could I do? We were in the shower it seemed a short time and then we got out and he helped me dry off and put a tee-shirt and underwear on me. I began to become very disassociated in my mind. I didn't know what had just happened. I tried to act like it did not bother me but it did. I was in denial and wondered what else was going to happen to me.

He called me into the kitchen and asked me if I wanted some lemonade and I really didn't want it because I wet the bed a lot and I didn't want to stain a mattress. He insisted that I have some and he took a big pill out of a cabinet in the kitchen, crushed it up with a spoon and told me it was sugar. He stirred the pill up in my lemonade and gave me the glass. I drank some of it but he insisted that I finish it all. I did drink it all and then he told me it was time for bed.

Uncle Vic took me into his bedroom and he took off his underwear and sat on the edge of the bed and then he pulled me into the bed. He laid behind me and put his erection between my legs and I was so ashamed and embarrassed. I then passed out cold. I don't know what he did to me that night but I know I was sexually abused while I slept.

The next morning when I woke up, Uncle Vic was standing over me telling me it was time for me to go home. I was surprised that I didn't wet the bed. I got dressed and we left his apartment. When we got to my house, I went inside as fast as I could. For the first time, I was glad to be there. Uncle Vic started talking to my mom in the kitchen and I went off into the living room trying to wake up. I was really tired from what I know now, the drug that he gave me. I wanted to go into my room and lay down I was so tired. I stayed in the living room playing and then it was time for Uncle Vic to leave.

On his way out he asked me if I wanted to spend the night again and I said No! After he left, my mom asked me with a very mean voice if he touched me in any way. I thought she would punish me so I told her no. My mom went back into the kitchen and when she did, I wanted to tell her what happened but as a child, I could not find the words. I just let the situation go and tried to forget the whole thing had happened.

In time as I grew, things like that were not happening anymore because I thought it was that I was getting older. Later, when I was thirteen, Uncle Vic would show up at the house while my mom was working. He would come over and always grab at me trying to pinch my breast. I would pull away and tell him to stop. He began asking me if I wanted to drive his car. I said yes and I began driving. He would ask me for sex and I would tell him no. When I turned fourteen, he began buying me alcohol and cigarettes. After I would drink the alcohol, he would sexually abuse me.

I was driving, drinking and smoking while he was sexually molesting me. I would pull away and tell him no but it didn't work. Uncle Vic would keep trying and the fight was so tiring that I would stop fighting and he would have his way with me. I had no friends and Uncle Vic gave me my alcohol which was a way of escape for me from everything that was going on at home.

Every time he and I would go out, we would stop by the liquor store and he would buy me a pint of bourbon whiskey, Jim Beam and I would begin drinking while I was out driving his car. Uncle Vic would take me to a property that he owned in the country and there he would let me shoot his guns, smoke and drink. After I would shoot his guns, he would always sexually abuse me. I hated every minute of it but I could not make it stop. It was happening over and over again. I got tired of fighting and began feeling very sick inside of myself. My body was numb all over when he was doing these things to me so I didn't feel anything but discomfort. I didn't know what to do about it.

My grades in school were dropping and I began staying home to drink and listen to music. I would drink to stop feeling anything and if I were drinking, life was a little more tolerable. When I turned fifteen, I was in a fantasy world of my own. I day dreamed all of the time and began not even to live my life in reality. How could I tell my secret to someone? I just kept everything to myself.

One afternoon, I was waiting for my last class to end and I looked outside and saw Uncle Vic's car parked under a tree. He was waiting for me to get out of school. I turned to my teacher and told her that I didn't want to go home with him because he was sexually abusing me. I shared my secret at last. She told me she would give me a ride home. She did and when we got to my house, Uncle Vic was there waiting for me. My teacher pulled up in the drive way, let me out of the car, said good bye and drove away. When I got in the house, he gave me alcohol, I got drunk and he sexually abused me like always.

One afternoon while I was driving his car, he told me he wanted to go shoot his gun. We went to his property in the country and began shooting his pistol. We were shooting at my empty beer cans. As I was shooting, Uncle Vic bent down to pick up my beer can to put it in a log near the lake. I took aim of the gun to the back of his head. I put my finger on the trigger and told myself to kill him. I thought about sending him to hell before his time and when he stood up, I lifted the gun from his head. I wanted to shoot him but changed my mind. The idea that I could have killed him made me feel a great deal of power over the situation and I felt for the first time in control over what was happening.

When we got back to my house, my mom was home and when we walked in, my mom could tell I had been drinking. I walked past her and went to my room. I laid down on my bed and tried to sleep. My mom came into my room and wanted to smell my breath. I let her and she went back into the dining room. I heard her ask my Uncle Vic if he had given her kid alcohol and he said he only gave me a little bit. My mom never said anything to me about it. She just let the situation go.

As an adult, at times, night after night I tried to figure out a way to kill him when I was younger and wondered if I could have gotten away with it. I could have said that I was drunk and tried to shoot the beer can out of his hand and missed. I wondered if it would have worked. I knew I could be tried as an adult for murder and maybe do twenty-five years. I was almost willing to do that. I would be out of prison when I was around forty years old. I wouldn't have to work in prison to pay any rent or a mortgage. Free food, clothing, medical. I might have been able to survive twenty-five years in prison. The thought stayed with me for some time but God enabled me to forgive him, eventually.

One morning I was in my room and I heard the phone ring. My mom answered and after she hung up the phone, she told me that Uncle Vic had cancer. I was so happy to hear that. I figured now he could die on his own. I would be free soon.

My Uncle Vic died about six months later. I was sixteen at the time and was very happy about his death. My night mare had ended and I felt so much relief for a change. I wasn't aware of the fact that a lot of damage had been done to me. I still stayed in my fantasy world and would continue to drink and smoke. The pain wouldn't go away though. I felt so violated and stopped taking care of myself. I just didn't care about anything anymore. Then I began to tell myself that I didn't care and it didn't affect me at all. I was just a sex toy and I didn't mean anything to anyone. It took years for me to recover from that trauma and it is something I will never forget. It would take God's help to restore my life and make me feel that I was a whole person. Later on, in my life, God did heal my pain and shame that I had deep inside of myself. All I feel God has said to me about it, is that it wasn't my fault that these things had happened to me.

Now in my life God is trying to help me forgive, once again, the things that Uncle Vic had done to me. I love God and know if I forgive, it is good for me. I believe it helps me to heal from the deep hurts inside of me. I talk to Jesus about it and he is always faithful in listening to me. I believe because of these things, if I survived, maybe others would see that they can survive too. Our God is a God of restoration and love. He is always faithful and loves us unconditionally.

I never told my mom the things that were done to me. The way that her life was going, I didn't want to make her feel worse inside. I had learned about sex the wrong way at a very young age. The situation that I was in caused me to be very confused about sex. Marriage is a very special thing that enables a couple to express love to one another. Maybe one day in my life I might have that. We will see what God does.

As a teenager, at sixteen I began dating guys. It was the thing to do and every one had a boyfriend, that I knew. I never really liked guys and couldn't stand it when they would put their hands on me. I really didn't like sex either but everyone was doing it and I cared nothing about myself so why not do it, it was the thing to do when I was younger.

I tried to function like everyone around me but always felt out of place. I had a lot of severe depression and stayed in my room most of the time. I listened to a lot of music during these times and would mow my grandmother's grass in order to save money to buy music albums. I listened to rock bands mostly and tried to drink when my mother wasn't home during the week working. I would stay in a fantasy world all of my own and it helped me escape everything that was going on in my life.

The only friends that I seemed to have lived down the street and I would often go to their house and talk mostly to my friend's father. We talked about all sorts of things and he knew everything that was going on in my life. I had found a new friend.

The days that I would cut school, I would go to my friend's house and talk with their father, John, all of the time. He was an insurance sales man and went to work later in the mornings, about eleven am. John began after a while, making sexual advances towards me.

He and his family were moving to Florida and they asked me if I wanted to ride there with them. It was about an eight-hour drive from South Carolina. I asked my mom if I could ride down with them in the summer of that year and she agreed to let me go with them. I was sixteen at this time and looked forward to the trip to Florida with John and his family.

The time came to go to Florida and John packed a truck with all of their furniture and things. His wife would follow us in her car and my friend's boyfriend would drive his car.

When we got to their new home, John continued to make sexual advances towards me and I just ignored him. I was happy to be away from home and felt that I could handle the situation. He kept pushing me to have sex with him and instead of losing my new friend, I let him have his way with me.

I felt afterward so sick inside and ashamed of what had happened between us. I wanted to go back home at that point. John had to drive back to South Carolina to do a few other things so I went with him. We acted as if nothing had happened but I could not forget about it. I was a minor and once again I felt violated. After John went back to Florida, we never spoke to one another again.

When I got back home, I took a summer job at a seafood restaurant near a bar that my mom and step dad went to all of the time. I worked on the weekends at night and my job was bussing tables. I really liked my job and made a lot of friends. I met a waitress there and she was a beautiful blond, blue eyed woman, the age of twenty-four years old. I was still sixteen and the owner of the restaurant, allowed us young girls to work at the restaurant for cash.

I really liked this waitress and loved her blue sports car. I asked her if I could have a ride in her car sometime and she asked if I would like to go to a movie the following Monday afternoon. I said that I would and she told me that would give me a chance to ride in her new car.

I found that I was very attracted to her and would think of her often. I couldn't wait until Monday and looked forward to seeing her.

Monday came and she picked me up at twelve thirty in the afternoon. She parked in our driveway and I ran out to meet her. We drove off and were running late. We got to the theater and walked in quickly. We got popcorn and went in to see the movie. We were seeing the first showing of the movie, Rocky and I looked forward to it.

The movie finally started and while we were looking at the movie, she put her leg on top of mine. I didn't know what to do so I just sat there not moving. She finally moved her leg off of mine and later the movie ended.

When we left, she didn't say anything about her leg being on top of mine and I wondered if she liked me in a physical attraction way. We got to my house and she told me that she would see me at work Saturday.

When I went to bed that night, I thought about the day and what she did to me. I liked it and wondered if something was wrong with me. I told myself that people didn't have relationships together with the same sex. I didn't at the time think they did. I changed my thinking as quickly as I could and tried to think of something else. I still couldn't stop thinking of her. I eventually fell asleep.

Saturday night at work, I didn't get the opportunity to speak with this waitress but wanted to very much. She was very busy and later when I did speak with her for a moment, she asked me if I would help her pack her things on Friday because she was moving. I agreed and she said that she would call me on Thursday to confirm. That night I wondered if she would make an advance on me on Friday. I would just wait and see. I told myself, if she did, I would respond to her.

Friday came and we went to her sister's house to pack her things, she was living there with her sister. We began to pack and we talked a while. She never made an advance toward me so after a couple of hours we left and she took me home.

She thanked me for helping her and drove off. I knew I would see her on Saturday night. I went in the house and thought about the day. I really liked spending time with her and again wondered about myself and my attraction to her. I thought people just don't feel this way about the same sex. At that point I thought something was wrong with me.

Later, due to peer pressure, I quit my job. Me and the other girls didn't like the way we were being treated at work so we decided to leave. It had been a while since I talked to my waitress friend and figured I would see her outside of work. I only talked with her a few times after I left my job and then we lost touch with one another. I decided I would look for another job.

CHAPTER

4

In the summer of 1981, my step dad's father died in a car accident. I was seventeen at this time and we inherited a vegetable field from his father. The field was over the fence from our back yard. I had the job of plowing up the dirt with a tractor. We grew vegetables, water melon and cantaloupe. We loved the melons and we used to pick them in the summer.

When my mom and step dad were home on the weekends, which wasn't very often, they would go into the field to pick the vegetables. We would have a good dinner when my mom decided to cook for us and we ate a lot on these particular weekends. My mom and step dad would drink at home.

I tried to figure out why I was still suffering from severe depression on these weekends when my mom and step dad stayed home. I couldn't think and stayed in my fantasy world. For some reason my depression was getting worse. I decided I would drink alcohol to feel better so my boyfriend and I would drive out to the field and party there in his blue Chevrolet truck.

We would listen to music and he would smoke his pot and I would drink. I didn't really like my boyfriend very much but I dated him because everyone dated and it was the thing to do. I hated it when he would touch me when we partied and wanted my fix from the alcohol only. After we would party a couple of hours, I would ask him to take me home. When I would get home, I would shut out the world and listen to music.

I felt really sick inside of myself and wondered what life would mean to me if I had a good friend or someone in my life, I could talk to about the things that were happening to me in my life. It was hard and I was all alone. I didn't make friends very easily and one of the friends that I did have beat me up at the school bus stop and broke my nose.

I couldn't understand why my thoughts were so different from the other people that were around me. I just didn't see things like other people did. I always lived in a lot of fear and my fantasies helped me escape from all that was in the world. I knew as a teenager, things just weren't right in my head. I knew there was a God and needed his help.

I felt really very helpless and wondered what life would be like as I grew into adulthood. I continued to drink alcohol and always felt better when I was buzzed or drunk.

I know now that God was looking out for me and taking care of me or I would have died from suicide. I thought about it a few times, I believe and sometimes felt all would be better if I had died. I prayed in my own way, I guess, the best I knew how.

I began seeing a drug counselor that worked at a detox hospital. Every time I would go and see her, the doctor there would take a urine sample before I would leave to go home. The doctor called my mom and told her that there was always a lot of alcohol in my system. My mom decided to put me in the hospital to detox the alcohol out of me. I felt she needed it not me.

I guess she just wanted to prevent my life from being like her life. I didn't like it but went along with it. I felt relived from the thought of not being at home.

My mom took me to detox on a Friday and we waited about an hour to sign me in. Once I was in the hospital, I noticed that there wasn't anyone there my age. I made friends with a woman there that was a recovering heroin addict and she seemed to be doing fairly well.

There were others in the hospital that were a lot older than myself and my friend I made there.

All I did in the hospital is watch television, played cards, listened to music and smoked cigarettes. I waited for withdrawal symptoms and never had any. Everyone was surprised by that. I felt that I wasn't an alcoholic I just drank for the fun of it and because I felt I needed it for my depression.

I was in the hospital for two weeks and ready to leave on a Wednesday afternoon. When I left the ward that I was in, a lady was there with my mom and they took me into a conference room. After we sat down and began to talk, the lady there told me that my mom and she were going to put me in a half-way house for recovering addicts. The place was for teenagers, boys and girls and it was called the Mason House.

I didn't want to go but the lady and my mom told me that if I refused that they would have a Judge put me there. I figured a Judge would put me in the home longer than if I volunteered to go, so I went with the lady. I didn't even say goodbye to my mom because I was so angry about the situation.

Outside in the parking lot was a bus with other kids in it and the lady told me that I would be going to the Mason House on the bus. My mom was outside waving at me goodbye but I ignored her and looked away.

There were a lot of kids on the bus of all ages. I felt really uncomfortable on the bus and no one sat with me. It was a long drive to North Charleston and I thought the Mason House would be closer to home.

When the bus got there, I got off the bus and went into the office and they said that they would show me where I would be staying. The rooms were in small cottages and looked like apartments inside. I was going to stay with two girls older than I was. They were hard core addicts, meaning they used strong drugs. I just used alcohol never anything stronger than that. I tried pot a few times but it made me paranoid.

The two girls introduced themselves to me and asked why I was there. I told them alcohol and lied and said that I used other drugs to look cool in their eyes. They said that the staff would show me around later after dinner.

At dinner time I met a few other people and they seemed to me like they had other problems too. There was a lot of talk about partying and some of the guys talked about girlfriends. They also had a pool table and stereo system for record albums in a play room. We listened to a lot of rock music and sat around and talked.

We had chores we had to do and I was to wash dishes after we all had a meal. I also found out that the bus in the mornings would drive us to school. I hated school and had one more year to turn eighteen and drop out of school. I didn't know that my life would change at eighteen years old for the better.

There was a guy at the Mason House named Randy. He had black wavy hair, brown eyes and I thought he was cute. He liked me and I wasn't really interested in him but he decided that he wanted me to be his girlfriend. I didn't really like him very much, I had other interests and didn't want to go steady with anyone. He kept bothering me about it, so I said that I would be his girlfriend.

We seemed to get along fairly well together but then later, I told him I didn't want to be his girlfriend anymore. He got really upset and went into his cottage room.

Later while we all were having dinner, except Randy this guy ran into the office and told the staff to call for an ambulance. They called 911 and said that Randy had slashed his wrists. The ambulance got there and the paramedics went into the cottage. Later they came out and said that Randy didn't cut himself very deep and that they put bandages on his wrists. They recommended counseling for him.

That night at a later time, Randy wanted to talk with me so we went into a sports trailer where they kept baseballs, bats, balls and basket balls for recreation purposes. Randy became very angry at me and grabbed a baseball bat and started hitting a wooden chair. The chair splintered into small pieces and Randy kept slamming the chair with the bat.

I ducked under a pillow on the sofa in the trailer and covered my face and head. All I could hear was yelling and the sound of the bat. I was very afraid and realized I could never have any kind of a relationship with anyone who would lose control like he did.

The day came after I had been at the Mason House for about two months, a guy there decided to put his hands on me in a sexual way. I was washing dishes and he came up behind me and started touching me all over my body. I told him to stop and chased him outside. There was a brick outside so I picked it up and threw it at him. It missed and hit a trash can and dented it.

Because I destroyed property, I was told to call my mom and have her pick me up the next day, in the morning. I was being kicked out of the Mason House. I was so happy and it was a weekend so I called my mom at her favorite bar and while she was drunk, I told her what happened and she said she would pick me up in the morning.

I was so happy packing. I knew I had to go home to a bad situation but I wanted my freedom back.

My mom did show up in the morning and we left. My mom didn't really say much to me, but when we got home, she said that she was happy to have me back. I just got my things out of the car and went inside to my room to listen to my music. I felt like I had to get out of my home as soon as possible and started thinking about how.

A drug counselor I knew her name was Sandy, told me I needed to get out of my home. she asked if I had anywhere to go and I told her, no I didn't think so. She asked about my Dad. I told her that I never considered it because I never seen my Dad very much. I also told Sandy that my dad had remarried and that I didn't think his wife would want me there. She told me to ask him if I could stay with him anyway.

I thought about it for a while and then called him. Dad answered the phone and I just told him a little about what was going on and asked if I could live with, he and his wife, Robbie. My dad told me that he would call me back and let me know what Robbie says about the situation. My dad did call me back later and told me that she said it was okay to do. I was eighteen at the time and felt it was time to try and get a job and get out if my home.

One night on a weekend before I moved, I heard screaming at about three o'clock in the morning. My mom and step dad were in the bathroom and I heard my mom yelling that my step dad was about to break her arm. I stayed in bed because I was tired of all of the fighting that was going on in the house. Screaming continued until much later and then the problem was over.

I began thinking about shooting my step dad. I could say it was self-defense. We had a 12-gage shot gun and a 410-shot gun. I could load one night while they were out and wait for them to come home. After I thought of it for a while, I could see that it was premeditated murder and decided not to shoot him. It wasn't worth prison to me so the thought left me. Sometimes I wonder what would have happen if I did shoot him.

Little did I know that after I would be with dad for three years, I would leave my family and South Carolina and my life would become much worse than it was ever!

My mom and dad talked about my depression and thought it would be good for me if I stayed at a psychiatric hospital before I moved in with my dad. I agreed and my dad talked to the staff at the hospital and they decided I would come to be registered and taken in sometime on the weekend.

My depression was bad and I tried to act as if nothing was wrong with me. I also began to get congestion and a cough that was pretty bad. My dad picked me up on a Saturday and I had one suit case with my things in it. My mom didn't really buy me a lot of clothing and most of the time I wore my sister's jeans. She was smaller than me so they really didn't fit very well, but I wore them anyway.

My dad, I and Robbie went to the hospital and while they were trying to check me in, they told my dad that his insurance wouldn't cover my stay there. My dad was surprised by that so we ended up leaving the hospital and we drove to my new home, dad's house.

When I got into the house, they showed me my room and when they did, I told Robbie that I had to lay down because I was so sick. Turned out I had the flu and I have never been as physically sick in my whole life. I finally asked my dad to take me to the hospital.

He called Robbie at work and she rushed home and they took me to a doctor. The doctor gave me a shot, I think for congestion and then they took me home and put me in bed. About two weeks later I began to feel better.

I wondered where I could get a job. My dad said that if I stayed there with them, I would have to go to school or get a job. My aunts cut hair so I decided I would try that so I enrolled in beauty college in down town Charleston.

I had to take a math test so on a Saturday Robbie took me down to the school and I took the test. I did pass and started school the following Monday.

On the day that I started school I had to do a haircut with instruction on a white man. I tried to follow instructions but needed help so a student there finished the haircut. The student told me I should have tried to finish the haircut because she got a five-dollar tip. I was upset but I learned to cut hair shortly after that.

I went to school Monday thru Friday and on the weekend's dad, Robbie and I would go to her parent's house in the country, Harley Ville, South Carolina. I loved it there. Robbie's father raised cattle for beef and I liked feeding them grain. They were neat I thought and I got to pet them too.

My life was a lot different than living in the hell I was in. I felt happy for a change and it was nice. I never dreamed my life could change so much for the better but it did.

At school I met a man that was a homosexual. I never met anyone who was gay so being around him was new for me. I wondered once again if I was gay and thought I might be because of the feelings I have had for women. I always thought something was wrong with me but seeing this guy, I made up my mind that I was gay.

This gay man was a white guy and wore some eye makeup and dressed nice and always carried a purse with him. I watched him do women's hair and thought he did a really good job. I wondered what his life was like and wondered if he had a boyfriend. I decided that I wanted a girlfriend and tried to figure out how to get one. I told myself that I would wait a while before I would look for a girlfriend.

The day came that I graduated from the beauty college and was ready to go to the state board to take the exam for a cosmetology license.

The state board was in Columbia South Carolina so when I did go, I had to drive. It was about two hours away from where I lived. I had to take a neighbor friend, female with me and cut and style her hair to be graded. I also did hair color applications with toothpaste.

My test results came in and I failed finger waving so I got a plastic head with hair from a beauty store and began practicing on it. My step mom, Robbie said I could do the waves and to keep trying. I eventually got it and passed the board exam and got my license. Now it was time to look for a job.

CHAPTER

5

I began going to an Episcopal Church with my dad and I really liked it there. I only worked during the week at a hair salon so my Sundays were free. We had Bible study on some of the mornings and I met an elderly man and wife who were wonderful people. After we got to know each other fairly well, the wife came into my job for a haircut and invited me to dinner at their house. I accepted. She gave me the directions to her house and as we were talking, she began to talk with me about the baptism of the Holy Spirit.

Before I finished her haircut, she told me to ask God for that baptism. I told her I would and that I would see her at her house on Friday afternoon. When I got there to her house the husband began telling me all the things that the Holy Spirit would tell him about and teach him. After dinner they asked me if I had asked for the baptism of the Holy Spirit and I said yes. At that moment they stood up and the husband placed his hands on the top of my head and began to pray in a foreign language.

The top of my head felt like strong electric shocks. I didn't really know what was going on at the time, but knew it was a spiritual thing that was happening. Afterward I felt really good and I believe this prayer was to help me endure all the trauma that was going to be coming into my life in the future. After they finished praying for me, I said goodbye to them and went home wondering about the night and the prayer, what it meant. A couple of days later I tried to go to their house, they lived in a trailer and I couldn't find their home. I drove around and looked for them and I couldn't find them.

I thought it was awful strange that I couldn't find them. Later that Sunday morning the elderly couple came to church and said that they were moving. They told me that they do what the Lord tells them to do and that they believed that it was time to go. They were only in South Carolina for less than a year. I knew I would miss them. They were like grandparents to me.

My mom introduced me to a lady who taught meditation on scripture in the bible. My mom said that she told her about me and she wanted to know if I wanted to have sessions with her. I said that I would and my mom gave me her number. I called and we agreed to meet after I got off of work at the hair salon, I worked at on a Thursday night at seven. She gave me directions to her house.

Thursday night came and I met this teacher at her home. I found out that she was just house sitting and that she traveled a lot teaching the meditation on scripture. We began reading the bible and she would ask me what I would see in my head after reading. I would tell her thoughts that I had that were irrelevant to the bible. It didn't really make a whole lot of sense to me during these sessions.

After a couple of months, I told her that I wanted to end our sessions and she agreed. I told her I would like to remain friends and she said okay but that she was traveling somewhere else and I asked her where and she told me that she didn't know. She was just going to go somewhere. I thought it was strange but felt she knew what she was doing so I told her goodbye and I went back home. I told my dad a little about her.

My mom had served my stepdad divorce papers but they were still living together. My mom had a friend at work, Don and they had coffee together every morning before they would go to work. They became really close and would talk on the phone all of the time. They became really good friends. Don knew a lot about my mom's life and would talk to her about things like that. Don was about twelve years older than my mom and had already got gray hair. He also had a short gray beard. I thought he looked really cool and I liked him a lot.

At this time my mom was thirty-eight and Don was fifty. One afternoon I went to my mom's house to see my brother and my brother and former step dad were there. My former step dad was showing my brother how to cook a dove that my brother shot. The phone rang and I answered it. It was my mom and she said that she was going to marry Don that night and to get my brother, Jim and bring him to her to Don's apartment. She then asked to speak to my step dad.

I knew that it was going to be a bad thing in the house. I handed the phone to my step dad and after a few minutes he began yelling and telling my mom to get home now. He then hung up the phone and went into the bedroom and was looking at the shot guns in the closet. I asked him what he was doing and told him it wasn't worth it. He began crying and asked me what was he going to do now. I told him I didn't know and after he calmed down a little, I tried to get my brother to go with me to Don's apartment but he wouldn't leave with me.

I called my mom and told her that Jim wouldn't come with me and that my step dad had left. My mom came and picked up my brother and asked if I would come to her wedding that night. I told her I guess I would. I felt like Don was her way out of the situation she was in and that she wasn't thinking clearly but anything was better than what she had I thought.

I went back home to dad's and told Robbie that my mom was getting married and I needed to get dressed. Robbie asked if we just got notice and I said yes. I got dressed as fast as I could and made it to the apartment. One of my mom's woman friends was a Justice of the peace and she married them. I felt so bad for my mom and figured in time the marriage wouldn't work but I tried to be happy for her. That was her only way out and Don had given her an ultimatum at the time. I liked Don and felt that we would all adjust.

My mom eventually sold her house and gave my former step dad, her ex-husband half of the money. Later she and Don rented a house not far away from where my mom's house was and my brother and sister lived with them. I would often go to spend the night over mom and Don's house and it wasn't long before mom started drinking again.

Don was retired from the Navy and on the Air Base near where my dad's house was, our home they had meetings for alcoholics and their families. My step dad, Don asked me if I wanted to go to the meetings with, he and my mother so I said that I would go. Every night on Fridays at seven pm, Don and mom would pick me up over my dad's house and we would drive out to the air base to attend the meetings.

My mom had one meeting and Don and I would go to another room for a separate meeting for the families of alcoholics. I met a lot of nice people there. We would all discuss how to live in the environment with our alcoholic loved one. We all talked about our fears and concerns about drinking.

I met a lady there named Connie. She and I became good friends and I began to tell her that I thought I was gay. She told me that she had a friend in California, Jan that was gay and that maybe I should start writing her. Connie asked Jan if I could write her and Jan said that I could.

I wrote her and told her some things about myself and my life and she in exchange told me about herself. I learned that she had two children, a boy six years old and a daughter, four years old. Jan was divorced and said that she was gay and that she wanted to be in a relationship with someone. I told her that I did too.

After talking on the phone for a while we decided to get into a relationship with one another and that I would move out to California and live with her. I thought it would be a good idea so we made the arrangements by talking about it and I needed somehow to tell my parents that I would be leaving South Carolina. I was twenty at this time and Jan was thirty-five. I was too young to be making a decision like the one I was making but it didn't matter to me at the time. Someone actually said that they loved me. That was all I needed to hear.

When I told my mom and dad I was moving to California, they were shocked and asked me where I was going when I got there. I told them with a friend I met by letters. My dad asked me also how I was going to get there and I told him I was going to drive my car. He said that I wasn't taking the car anywhere. I then told him that I would take the bus.

He was upset about my going away and I think my parents just thought I was talking and not serious about moving. I talked to Jan on the phone and told her that my dad took my car away so I would take the bus and she said that she would pay for a flight. I said no to her and made arrangements to take a Grey Hound bus.

The day came that I was leaving and my dad was on his way to work. He kissed me and told me to have a good trip and to call him when I got to California. I told him that I would and he left the house.

I went into my room and checked my suitcase to make sure that I was bringing the things that I wanted to bring and all was okay. I waited for my mom to pick me up to take me to the bus station and I was excited about my trip.

My mom was a little late getting to the house I thought and then the phone rang. It was my mom on the other end of the phone and she was drunk. She said that she didn't want to take part in me throwing my life away and that she wasn't going to give me a ride to the bus station. I hung up on her and quickly called my sister and told her that I needed a ride. She said that she would come and pick me up.

My sister got to my house just in time to get me to the bus station. We got there and my sister said goodbye to me and drove off. I waited for the station to call my bus number and then I boarded the bus. I sat down in a middle seat and looked around at down town Charleston. I thought that I would miss the city but wanted to go. There was no turning back now.

The bus pulled away from the station and I was on my way to California. At this time, it was in May of 1985 and I was twenty years old and I only had sixty dollars in my pocket.

Jan was to pick me up in Ontario California in three days. She lived in Diamond Bar California and I looked forward to living there. I heard that it was a beautiful place and there were lots of hills near by Jan's home. I wondered what I would do for working a job. I decided not to worry about it and that I would find something to do like working in a grocery store or something like that. I put my jacket against the bus window and fell asleep.

The bus ride was a long one. It was a three-day journey and the buses that I was on kept stopping at a lot of bus stations in different states. We had to change buses all of the time and I think that is what made my ride so long a trip. I took baths in bus station bathrooms and ate a lot of hamburgers at Burger King restaurants. I couldn't wait to get to California because I was so tired.

I made it to Ontario California and Jan was waiting outside when our bus pulled up at the station. I gave her a hug and when we got in the car, we talked all the way to her house. I liked the house. It was a greenhouse with a beautiful front yard. The grass was so green and well kept. Her two children were at their baby sitter's house and Jan said that she would pick them up later.

We went inside and talked some more. Later we went to get her kids and they were adorable children. Dark skin, black hair and eyes. Their father was black and Jan was white. Jan had a 6-year old boy and a 4-year old girl. Jan and her husband were divorced before her daughter was born. I would meet he ex-husband later.

After some time, I was there, about a month, I decided I wanted to get a job. My cosmetology license wasn't good in California so I had to apply for the California state board in order to take the test there. In the mean time I worked at the Mall in a cookie store. I made cookies all day long and Jan would pick me up from work every day. I made a little money for spending but not nearly enough.

Jan said in order to get a good job in California, I would have to get my GED and then a job there for the state or government. I didn't have a college degree so it would take some time to find something in California. I wanted to work for the Government but in the meantime, I took the test for my cosmetology license and passed. I worked in several beauty shops but never felt I was making enough money there. I applied to take my GED test at an adult school in Rowland Heights California.

I passed my GED and started looking for work. I took and job at K-Mart and worked in their patio department. The job was okay but they didn't pay very much but I decided I would stay there for a while.

CHAPTER

6

In February, 1987 I was twenty-two and things seemed to be going okay with my job and at home with Jan and the kids. I was thinking about going to college and took a few classes at Cal State Fullerton. I wanted to get a degree in Psychology and work as a therapist. That didn't work out well because I realized I was the one needing help so I dropped the classes. I continued working in the patio department at K-Mart and would look for work somewhere else at a later time.

One night at four o'clock in the morning the phone rang. I picked up the phone and my dad's voice was on the other end. He told me to wake Jan up and I lied and said that she was up already. My dad told me that my mother had a car accident and died. I was in a state of shock but not surprised at all about the situation. My dad said that they would have to get a plane ticket and fly me home. I said that would be good and I hung up the phone.

I then called my sister and she was in shock and crying. I tried to comfort her and told her that I was coming home right away. We hung up the phone and I started to pack my things to take with me.

Jan and I decided that she would go with me, so we took the kids to their grand-parents' house and we were later that night on a plan flying to South Carolina, home.

My dad picked us up at the air port and took us to my sister's home and we stayed there overnight. The wake would be the next morning. I was really tired because I was on a plan all night and couldn't wait to go to bed. I thought about my mom's accident and couldn't get the thought out of my head. I finally did fall asleep and it was about 3am.

The next day I found out that there was an 18-wheeler staled on a bridge and my mom ran right into the back of it. The hospital said that her alcohol limit was very high and I figure maybe my mom passed out and hit the truck. She was drinking and driving, coming home from a bar that I found out that she had worked at. She also had a passenger in the car with her. He was in a comma at the hospital. My sister went to see him at a later time.

We all got in the car to go to the funeral home and I knew that I had to see my mom's body in a casket and I was nervous about it the whole way there. We finally got there and parked the car. I held my sister's hand and we walked in. Just before we entered the room where my mom's body was, we held our breath.

My mother was lying in a light blue casket. I was devastated and at that point stopped feeling anything inside of myself. I felt sick inside. My mom had a bruise on her chin that the funeral makeup couldn't cover completely. I could smell the formaldehyde that was in her body.

I no longer felt any pain or anger I just went numb inside. My mom was adopted and some of her family was there so I talked with them for a while. My brother was crying really hard and he was just sixteen at the time of my mom's death.

I talked with him and we went outside to smoke a cigarette. I told him that mom was okay and it would get better in time.

We left the funeral home a few hours after being there. I was ready to go home. I wanted out of South Carolina and to go back to California as soon as possible. It was a horrible experience that our family was going through.

The next day was the burial. We got to the funeral home at about one o'clock in the afternoon. My mom's friends read a poem and a pastor said a few things then my mom's casket was carried and put into the Herse outside.

We followed the Herse to the cemetery and the weather outside was awful. It was raining and they had a water pump in the ground pumping water out of mom's grave. I thought about my mom's accident and wondered what it was like for her to come out of her body. I wondered if she had felt anything on collision.

After she was lowered into the ground, as the dirt was being shoveled into the hole, I felt like it was sad that a forty-two-year-old who lived like she did, lost her life. I felt that it was over and everyone had to get back to life now without her. We left the cemetery and went to one of mom's friend's house.

All my mom's friends did was drinks alcohol. They began making fun of my dad so, we didn't stay very long. When we left, I was exhausted and ready to go to sleep.

Jan and I stayed a week and then flew back to California. I was glad to be home. I went back to work right away hoping to forget all that had happened. I couldn't get the accident out of my mind. I tried hard to forget and get on with things to do in my life.

As time went by, I began to feel very sick inside of myself. I was very depressed and frustrated. I was also having a hard time paying my bills because I couldn't find a job that payed enough money to support myself. I didn't know what to do. I was in and out of different jobs and wasn't happy with what I was doing.

I decided I would have to try anything to get a better job. I thought about the Postal Service so I paid for a class to learn about the test they offered to get hired there. I began studying for the test and began applying to take the test. I went to the library and got a book on Postal Exams and learned about memorization of numbers and addresses.

I began to receive test dates and times in the mail and started taking the tests. I scored very high on the tests and in time was called in for several interviews. I was offered a job in automation working nights. We sorted mail in machines by zip codes. Finally, I had enough money to make ends meet. I was very happy in my job but very sleepy all of the time.

I tried to sleep during the day but it was hard with the kids being home in the afternoons. A lot of noise all of the time. It was hard to get any rest but I knew I had to adjust. I needed the money because Jan and I talked about me moving out. We all had our own rooms and we were no longer in a relationship. She wanted me to move because she wanted a relationship but I wanted it to end.

We wanted to remain friends and I began looking for a place to go.

I met a gay man at work named Paul and he wanted a roommate to share a condo he was renting in Long Beach California. I was excited and told Jan about my offer. I told her that I would be living on the beach and that she and the kids could come over on the weekends. She thought moving there would be a good idea to start out being on my own. I was twenty-five at this time.

In Long Beach we did a lot of partying on the weekends. There were a lot of gay bars and Paul and I would go to these bars to drink and dance. I began not to feel very good about the things I was doing. I felt really sick because of the alcohol and I wanted pretty much to be left alone.

Paul always had lots of people over to party and to have fun. I was more of a quiet person at home and tried to sleep during the day. We worked at night and I was very tired. I began going to the Beach in the summer to lay out in the sun and get a tan.

It was really the only way I could get some rest. I liked going to the beach and the people were very nice there. I was able to rest a bit.

In the mornings I used to go to a small gay bar across the street from us and I would read the paper and have coffee. They had pool tables there and I always loved to play pool so I had fun.

I would also go to the small shops downtown Long Beach and look inside at all of the arts and crafts these small shops were selling. They were beautiful pieces of art. Shells glued on wood, a lot of wood work, tables and all kinds of things. It was nice just walking around.

I began feeling very sick inside of myself and I would scratch the skin off of my face with my finger nails. In the mornings I would look it the mirror and there would be soars all over my face. I told people at work that I was taking karate and that in tournament I would get hit in the face.

I felt like I was doing it for attention but with my thoughts in my head, I knew that I was sick and needed to see a psychiatrist really soon. I was seeing a counselor at the time and told her I was in fights in Long Beach. I didn't know really why I was doing this to myself but I felt better inside if I would mark my face with soars.

I believe this was the beginning of my psychosis but with a little help with other trauma events in my life later, my psychosis would get worse in time.

Jan and her daughter would come over to the condo on the weekends and we would have some fun. Paul and I were having some problems at the time but I figured it could be worked out if we talked some about the people always coming over to the condo to visit him all of the time.

I needed to rest and at work I had a hard time staying awake. I knew that eventually I would have to make some changes in my life but I didn't really want to think about it very much.

I needed to get out on my own and the thought scared me some. I was straight from dad to this new place in California and at times wish I had never moved here.

Time came in Long Beach for a gay parade down town. Every gay person it seemed in the area went to this parade. On the Beach there were a lot of booths with gay things for sale. Lots of rainbow flags and shirts. I looked around in all of the shops and found nothing that I really wanted so I didn't stay on the beach long. I drank some alcohol and tried to have a good time.

On that night the parade began with marching down the streets. As I was walking down the sidewalk, I approached a church behind a fence and there were people holding signs stating that it was sin and to repent. I held up my middle finger to give them a foul jester and a man with a camera from a popular magazine snapped my picture and I was happy about it.

I wanted people to know how I felt and what at the time that I was. I was hoping that the Christians would go away and leave us alone. After all, I loved God and felt that he loved me regardless of what I was. I kept walking and had a good time that night. Later I went home and thought about my life. I wanted to change and wanted to have a family I thought. The idea stayed with me for some time.

I called my sister in South Carolina on a weekend and we decided I should fly home for a visit. I told her I would make arrangements and call her back in a couple of days. I told Paul that I was going home for two weeks and that he could use my truck while I was gone.

I made the arrangements and, on a weekend, flew to South Carolina and stayed with my sister most of the visit.

I called Paul after I had been with my sister for a week and asked him how things were there. He told me, not very good and I asked him what was wrong. He told me that he would tell me when I got back. I asked him if he crashed my truck and he said no. He told me to enjoy my visit and not to worry. I worried but tried to forget about our conversation.

I had a good time with my sister and her two children. She had a girl and a son. We went out to the market places in down town Charleston and I just loved it. I missed South Carolina and my family.

I saw my dad a few times and then had to say goodbye to them and come back to California. While I was about to board the plane, I looked at my dad and waved goodbye and started my journey back to my home. I looked forward to getting back to see what Paul had to say to me about what was wrong.

When I got back home to the condo, I asked Paul what was wrong and he told me not to worried about it. I told him that I really wanted to know but he wouldn't tell me anything. I told him that I was tired and I went to bed.

The next day I wanted to go grocery shopping so I drove down to the bank to get some cash. I put my card in the ATM and I couldn't get any money out of the machine. I looked at the receipt and it said that I only had four dollars in my account. I couldn't understand what was wrong and went home and called the bank.

As I was on the phone with the bank complaining, Paul came out of the bedroom with a shoe box and inside were my checks and additional credit cards. He had mailed in papers that offered additional credit cards from the banks and started using them. He was buying jewelry and selling it to buy drugs. I didn't know that he was hooked on crack but he was. I tried to get two hundred dollars from a neighbor that Paul had bought drugs with but couldn't get the money back.

I went from store to store paying them the cash for my bounced checks. I also had Paul take me to all the stores in the Mall and return things that he had bought. I was really mad and felt very betrayed by Paul. I decided that I had to move out and called Jan and asked her if I could come back to her house in Diamond Bar for a while until I could find something else. She said yes so, I began to pack my things and wait for her to come over.

When Jan came over, she helped me pack my truck and I left Long Beach and moved back in with her and the kids. It was kind of nice to be back for a while. I slept pretty well that night because it was nice and quiet. I thought about what was done to me and I had never experienced anyone stealing from me before. I was still shocked and it took me a while to get over it.

I felt really sick inside of myself and continued to scratch soars all over my face. I just felt so bad inside and felt like I wanted the attention from others. I noticed a church near Jan's house and decided I would check it out. It was an Evangelical Free Church. I called them and asked them about gay people and how they felt about them.

All the church told me on the phone is that they were bible based and they followed what the bible said. I decided to go to their services. I went and really liked it there. I continued to go and ended up in a bible study group that I really liked and I began to feel better inside of myself.

I listened to bible tapes that my mom had bought for me for a birthday gift and was really getting very close to God I felt. I would sit next to the fire place at Jan's house and just meditate on scripture all day long.

I was able to quit smoking and I felt a lot of piece. I began to change for the better.

I had my own room at Jan's and wanted to stop my gay relationships because I felt I was in sin and wanted to live right before God's eyes. I'm not judging I just felt it was the thing to do.

I wanted to eventually get out on my own and started thinking about moving from Jan's house.

On night Jan's daughter was throwing a fit and I got involved with the situation. Jan's daughter was twelve years old and I should have left her alone but I didn't. She kicked me and we got into a fight. I should have gone to jail that night because I hit her back. We ended up on the floor and Jan came running into the living room where we were. I told Jan to go back in the other room and we continued to fight.

Finally, Jan's daughter bit me really bad on my arm so I let her go. She went to a friend's house to spend the night and I went to the emergency room so a doctor could check my arm. I asked Jan for a ride to the hospital and she said no to me because she was angry with me.

I didn't blame her after all it was her child I was fighting with. I felt a lot of anxiety and didn't think I could drive myself but I did.

The doctor at the hospital who examined me told me that I should move out that night or the next day. I think he was afraid that I would be arrested. I was twenty-seven at the time and it was illegal to hit a child. I decided to leave the next day.

I had a friend who worked in selling homes and renting apartments and she owned a few apartment homes in Fullerton California. They weren't far from where I lived and I told my friend that I had to move out first thing in the morning. She said that she would be at Jan's in the morning to help me pack my things and then we hung up the phone. When I went to bed that night, I felt really bad about what had happened and wish things were different than they were.

My friend showed up at eight o'clock in the morning and we put my things in my truck and her car. I had already packed that night and was already, ready to leave the house. My friend and I got to an apartment complex that she owned and it was a dump of a place but I moved in.

I thanked my friend and told her that I would pay her later on that week. I wanted an upstairs apartment so I picked one. It was tolerable so I moved my stuff in and started a new life on my own. I didn't know for the life of me that things would get really horrible in my new life alone.

I continued to drive to Diamond Bar to attend church there. I liked the bible study so much that I went as much as I could. It was a very nice church and all the people there were really friendly to me. I felt like I had a new family at church. The studies were great and I loved every minute of it.

While at work at the Postal Service I met a new employee named Willy. He was a black man at about the age fifty and we talked about the bible and the Lord. We became friends very quickly and we began going out to breakfast together in the mornings after work. He and I would get a lot of looks from other people because he was a black man out with a young white girl.

I told Willy that I wanted to move into a nicer apartment and asked him if he would help me look. We found one in Fullerton right down the street where I lived. It was a nice apartment so I put money down and the next day moved in. Willy helped me move and I was so happy to have a nice place. I had a one bed room and they had a pool so Willy and I did a lot of swimming.

It was summer and we had a blast at my apartment. Willy and I would sit outside in the shade at a table outside and have bible study together. I was happy that I had found a friend that I had something in common with. I didn't know that Willy pretended to be a Christian and he had bad plans for our friendship.

At church Willy would go with me to the bible study group and no one ever said anything about us being black and white or our age difference. I thought I had found the perfect friend.

After some time as our friendship grew, we met an elderly couple at church and they really liked us. The woman wanted to introduce me to her son, Donald. He was thirty years old and really needed some friends his mom told me. I agreed to meet him and Willy didn't seem to like the idea very much. Donald called me one weekend and we decided that he would come over to my place to go swimming. He did come over on a Saturday and I really liked him a lot. The only thing that bothered me is that he talked too much I felt. I couldn't really get a word in but I decided I would tolerate it. I wanted a boyfriend to love as much as normal as I could so Donald and I began dating one another.

Willy and Donald didn't like one another very much so I tried to keep piece between them. It was hard but I managed to talk with Willy about the situation so Willy stopped arguing with Donald.

The guys were at my apartment it seemed all of the time. I wasn't getting any sleep and Donald began spending the night while I was working. I worked from eleven pm until eight am. I was really tired. When I got home, I would sleep while Donald made his self at home. Donald wasn't working because he had a work injury so I was paying all of the bills by myself. At night Donald would run the air-condition all night and my electric bill was really high.

When I talked to Donald about it, he told me that I was a Christian and that I should open up my home to others that might need a place to stay. He began telling me that his roommate and he didn't get along very well and that he wanted to stay with me. I didn't want to but I told him that he could stay with me. It was a disaster and I was not happy at all.

One morning Willy and I were having breakfast and Willy asked me if I wanted him to go home with me and ask Donald to leave. I said yes so, we went to my apartment after we finished up eating.

I went into my apartment and Donald was sleeping. I woke him up and told him I wanted him to go home that I needed my space. Donald would not get up so I started yelling at him to get out. I couldn't take it anymore. I had no quiet time to myself.

Donald jumped up and started yelling and throwing things he grabbed me and just then Willy walked into the room. Donald was surprised to see Willy and began yelling and cursing. I was so afraid and thought that he was going to hurt me.

Donald began packing the few things that he had and Willy helped him take his belongings to his truck. Willy kept telling Donald that I only wanted my space for a while but I felt differently after Donald's fit, he threw. I was really afraid of Donald at this point and wanted him to leave me alone from now on.

When Donald came back into the apartment, he was yelling so loud and throwing things. The neighbors could hear Donald yelling and I was embarrassed. I told him I wanted him out and he wouldn't leave. Willy dialed 911 and Donald then left the apartment.

Willy hung up the phone and the dispatcher called me back and asked why I hung up the phone. I told her that I thought that my boyfriend was going to hurt me but that he had left. She didn't believe me so she sent a police officer to my place to check on me.

The police did come over and he decided to call Donald at his place and tell him not to come over to my place anymore. He did call and when the police officer hung up the phone, he told me to get a restraining order to protect myself. I agreed and the officer left the apartment. I asked Willy if he would stay with me a while to protect me from Donald. He said that he would.

I was able eventually to go to sleep. I was exhausted and needed to rest. Willy slept on the sofa.

Willy and I stayed away from church because Donald and his parents were going to the bible study that I belonged to, so we waited two weeks then I decided Willy and I should go back because we were part of the group there and I shouldn't be afraid to go anymore.

On the following Sunday after two weeks Willy and I showed up at church and in the parking lot Donald came running out and began pushing me as I got out of my truck. One of the men that attended the bible study with us told Donald to stop pushing me so he stopped. Willy and I walked into the church and sat down for service.

After the service Willy and I were a little afraid to go to the bible study but we went anyway. Donald and his parents were there at the study and I knew they would, they started saying all kinds of mean things to me and about me. His parents said that I was a horrible person and that I threw their son out of my apartment.

I didn't do any explaining I just let them run their mouth. A lady that was new to the group, who was part of the church, there to observe the study, told them to keep the problem outside of the church.

This woman went around the room and asked us each what we would like to study in the bible. When she got to me, I told her that I would like to study about the gifts of the Holy Spirit. I also told her I would especially like to study the gift of speaking in a spiritual language. I got some looks from the others in the group. We continued with the bible study.

When Willy and I got back to my apartment we talked about Donald and his parent's behavior toward me. We agreed that I needed to stay away from Donald outside of church. Willy and I decided to go swimming and forget the whole thing ever took place. We had a good remainder of the day and later went in late for bed time. I watched a little television and then went to bed. Willy slept on the sofa.

It was Monday morning and the phone rang rather early. We thought it was Donald so Willy answered the phone. It was the pastor from church and he asked to speak to me. I got on the phone and he said that I wasn't allowed to go to the bible study anymore. He also said that the church wasn't a Pentecostal church. I told him that I knew that and that the only reason we go to his church is for the bible study group.

He told me that he felt that I should find another church to attend. I hung up the phone and was devastated emotionally. I loved that bible study group. Willy told me that he was sorry and that we would find something else. I was so hurt that I went to bed and slept almost all day until time to go to work that night.

Donald kept calling the apartment cursing at Willy and asking to talk with me. I didn't want to talk with Donald so I wouldn't take his calls. I had a problem with Donald for a while and knew I would. In about three weeks Donald left us alone.

About a month later, I was feeling really sick and went to bed that night really early around six pm. I feel asleep very fast and when I woke up, I remember looking up at the ceiling and could not remember what my name was. I did not know what was wrong with me and I felt like I was on something like drugs. It took me a while to get my thinking back and I felt sick the rest of the night.

For the next couple of weeks, I felt really sick. I could not think clearly and my mind was really delusional. When it was around five pm, I told Willy that I wasn't going to work that night because I was really sick. For some reason Willy didn't seem to look very surprised and said that he would take the bus and that I didn't need to drive him there.

After Willy left, I could not sleep at all and decided to watch television for a while. When I turned on the television set, as I was watching it, I began to hallucinate. The picture had a dove flying out toward me and the people on the set were saying awkward things like the ark had been found and all kinds of things. I knew that the ark hadn't been found and wondered what was wrong with me.

After hallucinating for a while, the phone rang and when I picked it up it was Willy's voice on the other end. He asked me with great concern if I was alright and I asked why he was asking me. He said that he knew I wasn't feeling well and wanted to call me. I told him that I was fine and that I was going to bed soon. We hung up the phone and I tried to lay down a while.

I was in full blown mania and could not think very well at all. I thought that my hallucinating was God showing me things. I was out of my mind and didn't know what to do. I just sat at home trying to get my mind back. I started coming down a little after about six hours. I still had mania and could not sleep.

I was out of work about a week and wasn't feeling any better.

Willy came home from work one morning and he had a coffee for me. He handed it to me and I thanked him and took a sip of it. The coffee tasted like I had licked a stamp but I didn't think much about it and began to drink it. I began to feel really sick and told Willy that I was going to go to the Jacuzzi and relax a while. He didn't want me to go but I went anyway.

In the jacuzzi I began to hallucinate and felt really sick. A man that lived in the apartment complex saw me outside and told me that I looked really sick. I told him I was and I decided to go back to the apartment. I again thought that God was showing me things. I wasn't in my right mind and didn't know that I was being drugged by Willy.

I didn't sleep that night again and at this time I had been awake for three days. I did lay down though and tried to rest a while and felt that I was getting better. At this time, I had been out of work two weeks and I needed some kind of documentation or I had better get back to work. I was using my vacation time. I got five weeks a year.

In the morning I began to feel a little better and when Willy got home, we had bible study and then we went swimming. I was a little fuzzy headed but I was enjoying the swimming pool. I liked swimming and thought it would make me feel better than I had been feeling.

After being in the sun for a couple of hours, Willy and I decided to go back to the apartment to have lunch together. At lunch I began to tell Willy that I talked to a girl and that I liked her and thought I was gay. I thought I was over it but this girl brought back some gay feelings in me.

I also told Willy that I didn't want to ever have a relationship with a man again. Willy didn't like what he was hearing and told me that I was just confused because of what had happened with Donald. I told him no and that I had always felt the way that I did.

We talked a little more about it and we decided to sleep a while. I told Willy that I still didn't feel just right in my mind and that I wasn't going to work again that night. I had been out of work now for two weeks.

I gave Willy a ride that night to work and I went straight back home to try and sleep some more. I felt really sick again and didn't sleep that night. I began to get really delusional thoughts and thought that whales jumped out of the water so God could see them. I had other thoughts about defecting to Russia and that I was Russian and didn't belong in the United States anymore.

I'm not Russian and tried to figure out why I thought I was. Things didn't make sense in my mind. I bean to feel like I was melting and I knew I needed some help but who could help me I thought.

When Willy got home in the morning, we went out to have breakfast. I told him that I still wasn't feeling well and told him I should see a doctor. I also told Willy some more about the girl I liked and again Willy wasn't interested at all in what I was saying. I told Willy that I wanted a relationship with her and Willy got really upset.

We finished our breakfast and went back home. Willy slept and I listened to music for a while. The music sounded unlike music does. It had a chime sound and I thought the song was different than I have ever heard it before. I took my head set off that goes to my stereo and got some Kool-Aid that was in a pitcher in the refrigerator.

About three minutes after I drank the Kool-Aid I began to hallucinate again. I didn't understand why I was getting so sick and thought God was still showing me things.

That night I couldn't go to work because I was so sick. I was listening to music when Willy called me to the bed room. I went to the bedroom and Willy was holding a glass of Kool-Aid and told me to drink it because he was nice about getting it for me because he knew I didn't feel well.

I took the glass and drank some of the Kool-Aid. It was cherry and I didn't taste anything else in it. I finished the Kool-Aid and then I went back to my music. When I put my head set on, I began to feel a strong sexual desire. I didn't know what was wrong and thought it was just hormones because I hadn't had sex for a while.

After about one hour of this Willy said that he was leaving for work and I said good-bye to him. After he left, I grabbed my stomach and crawled to my room. Just as I got on to the bed I passed out. I slept the rest of the night. I didn't even think of work anymore because I was so sick all of the time.

I eventually put in vacation time at work again so that I wouldn't get written up for my attendance. I put in two weeks and tried to feel better by swimming and rest.

About two days later in the morning when Willy got home, he wasn't really talking to me very much. I asked him what was wrong and he said nothing was wrong. We talked a little when we went to the swimming pool and he mentioned my being gay. I told him that I always felt that way and that there was nothing I could do about it except be alone for the rest of my life. He agreed that was the best thing and then we changed the subject.

When we went back to the apartment, it was getting late. Willy called me to the bed room and when I got into the room, Willy threw me onto the bed and tried to force me to have sex. I put up a fight and he let me go. He told me that he was trying to help me change and I decided to go out onto the patio and tried to think of a way to get him out. I told him that he would have to find another place to stay.

He said that he wasn't leaving me. I then called the police and had him removed from my apartment. He stayed with one of his friends and thank God, he was gone.

It was a weekend and I decided to make something to eat. I had a full pitcher of Kool – Aid in the refrigerator and pored myself a glass. This time after a few sips, my apartment became a space ship and I was in the clouds escaping the fire judgment on the earth. The world was on fire and I looked into a mirror at my eyes and I turned into stone.

I fell onto the floor and I stopped breathing. I took a deep breath and stopped breathing again. Finally, I was able to breathe and I don't remember what else had happened. I just know I was really sick and life was intolerable for me.

Something told me to dump my Kool-Aid down the drain and I began to feel better after three weeks. Work didn't know where I was and I forgot that I had a job.

As I began to feel better things were melting and common sense hit me and I realized I had been drugged all of this time. I decided to drive myself to the emergency room which wasn't far from where I lived.

As I was driving the road was like waves on a beach that I was driving on. Street lights were very bright and I didn't know if I would make it to the emergency room. I did arrive and parked at the ambulance parking at the entrance of the hospital and I walked in.

I told the staff that I had been drugged and that I needed to see a doctor right away. They asked me what drug and I told them that I was hallucinating again and that I didn't know. I told them I thought it was LSD.

They checked me into the hospital and they took me to a room to wait for a doctor. I told them that I needed to see a doctor right then and couldn't wait any longer. A nurse came into the room and strapped me down by my leg to the bed. I asked her to please not strap my arms then she told me she wouldn't if I would be quiet. I told her that I would be quiet and she left the room.

I was hallucinating really bad and very delusional in my mind. My mind was racing and I couldn't slow it down. I was terrified. Finally, a doctor walked into the room. I told him what was wrong and that I was drugged. After talking with me for a while he said that I had a mental illness and that I needed to be admitted into a mental hospital. I kept telling him no that I was drugged.

The doctor called in a social worker and after she talked with me for a while the hospital put me on a hold against my will and had an ambulance pick me up and they drove me to a place called College Hospital. The ambulance driver walked me to a mental ward and talked with someone at a desk.

They told me that the doors were locked and that there was no need in trying to get out. I sat for a while in a recreation room and then a doctor came into the room and said that he was going to examine me. I told him that I was drugged and he told me that I was mentally ill and that hallucinating was part of the illness. I didn't care at that point I just wanted to get better.

The doctor said that they were going to keep me for about two weeks and that they were going to put me on a medication that would help me with the delusional thinking and the hallucinating. I said that would be fine and just make me better.

That night when it was time for bed, they gave me a drug called Haldol for schizophrenia. When I laid down after the lights were out, I began hallucinating and I could hear a lot of banging on the walls and screaming. I could not sleep.

Then all of a sudden, I could smell a vapor gas in the room and I got very dizzy so I grabbed a blanket that they gave me and laid down in the hall by my door and fell asleep there.

The next morning a nurse woke me up and told me to go back to bed and told me I couldn't sleep in the hall anymore. They came and woke me up to have breakfast and I told them that I wasn't hungry but they insisted that I try to eat something.

That morning it looked like everyone was wearing a wig on their head. I just could not get the hallucinating to stop. My mind was waisted and there was nothing I could do about it but just wait until the Haldol began to work. I began to realize I had a job and I needed to call and let my boss know where I was. The hospital said that they would call for me but they never did.

It was horrible in the mental hospital. The staff weren't very nice to us and treated me poorly. I couldn't wait to leave there and get back to my life the way it was before being drugged by Willy.

After about one week, I began to feel a lot better but the hallucinating was still happening once in a while. My mania was gone and I could sleep better but it was hard because I wanted out of the hospital.

After all of this, one night in the hospital, I was in my room and I shared a room with a girl there. I saw a green demon come into the room and it sounded like he was crushing bones with his teeth. I saw him sit on the girl while she slept and then laid down into her body. I was so scared and didn't know whether it was real or not. I finally went to sleep. It was scary.

One afternoon as I was sleeping, Jesus must have been in the room with me because I felt such peace after my horrible trial. I can't really explain it but every time I would wake up it felt like I was in ecstasy. It was wonderful. The nurse kept waking me up to talk with me about something. I told her I needed to go home to pay my bills. I signed release papers and a van took me back to the emergency room that I came from.

I figured by now they would have towed my truck but it was where I left it at ambulance parking near the entrance to the hospital. I felt as if God had helped me by not having my truck towed. I felt exhausted and worn out mentally. I drove home crying and wanted so bad for this trial to be over but it wasn't just yet.

I had quit smoking but when I got home, I bought a pack of cigarettes and lit up and took a big breath of smoked filled with nicotine. What a relief I felt and I wanted to get to work as soon as possible.

I checked my messages and my boss, Rob had called several times and told me that they couldn't find me and to call him as soon as I got his message. Apparently, my job sent the police over to the apartment to try and find out if I was okay. I calledRob and told him that a guy drugged me and that I was in the hospital. We talked a while and he said that I could return to work the next night. After I hung up the phone I laid down in my bed and fell asleep.

I was in severe depression when I woke up the next morning. I couldn't think because I was in shock and afraid, I would never get my mind back to the way it was, normal. I knew it would take a life time to get over this and it has taken that long. After my hospital trial, I walked away from the Lord. I didn't understand why God allowed me to suffer like this.

My brain was burned for life and I knew I would be on medication for what another person did to me. I challenged Jesus and told him that if he wanted me, he had the power to take me back to himself if he really loved me. I turned my back on God and tried to pick up the broken pieces of my life. Forever my life had been changed. I'll never forget it!

CHAPTER

7

Back at home I tried to live as normal as a life that I knew how. I was forever changed and knew I would have to start my journey away from God and on my own. I had not been at work for over two months and it was time to get back. I was able to pay my bills because I had taken vacation time and some paid sick leave to cover my expenses. I was still in shock and knew it would take forever to recover from that shock.

I didn't know what I would tell everyone when I got back to work on Monday. I cried a lot and was hoping that I did not cry at work. I was so depressed and this time it was clinical depression that required medication. I found a psychiatrist and was able to get refills on my prescriptions. I was taken off of Haldol and put on Lithium instead. Later I would take Depakote and Zoloft for depression and Mania. I kept asking God why?

I walked into work on Monday night and my eyes were dilated from my medications. Everyone at work said that they thought I was dead because no one knew where I was. I told them that I was sick and, in the hospital, that is all I said to them.

Every thing was blurry and I felt sick from all of the medication that I was on. I knew that my brain had been burned and I needed to take my medication so I suffered. I was in luck though because Willy was sent to another plant. Thank goodness for that. I probably would have shot him if I knew the magnitude as to what he had done to me.

My thyroid was wasted and destroyed from the drugs so, I was on medication for that too.

I wanted to believe that I was mentally ill and that this never happened to me it would have been easier, I thought, if I were. I was now mentally ill and had to learn how to make my life work in this condition. I didn't feel much of anything anymore in my emotions. I was in a dry state in my mind. My mind didn't work very well anymore and I started living in a fantasy, fiction world in my thoughts. I even believed some of my thinking.

As time went by, I was hospitalized on several more occasions due to the flash backs of the drugs that Willy gave me. I was torn inside and heart broken. The doctors told me that I would be on medication for the rest of my life and that is true so far.

I had to come to the realization that someone harmed me but I would have to let it go and to forgive in order for my life to work. This took a life time so far but I'm getting better at it as time goes by.

About six months later, one night I was laying in bed and we in California had a really big earth quake. I jumped up and my walls were shaking back and forth. I thought they were going to cave in and crumble. I ran under the door way of my room and waited for it to stop. Eventually, it did stop and my heart was racing with fear.

Right after my phone rang and when I answered a familiar voice was on the other end asking me if I was alright. I told her yes. She was a friend I met at work. Her name was June and she was about sixty, I was twenty-eight at the time. I told her that my apartment almost collapsed and that I would need to move out as soon as possible. She told me that we would talk about it at work.

I was ready to move out! Nothing but bad memories at home! I tried to think of where I could move to. I asked around but nothing came up. I was afraid of living where I was. We kept having aftershocks and I was really afraid of being at home alone. I needed to do something and do it fast.

June and I began talking at work. We agreed that I would need someone for a while to look after me to get me out of bed during my depression and to make sure I made it to work at night. I got documentation from a doctor requesting that the Postal Service change my hours due to my medical condition. They honored my doctor's request and put me on the same hours as June was on, four pm to twelve thirty am. It worked for me a little better with my sleeping schedule and I felt a little better too.

June told me while we were talking at work and she said that she and her husband had an extra room that I could stay in for a while until I got myself back together again. I said that I would like that so June said that she would ask her husband if I could move in. She said that she would call me that day and let me know his answer.

June did call and told me that her husband said that I could stay with them and I was so happy about that. I found out later never move into a friend's home with a husband around!

On a Saturday at my apartment, June and I began to pack my things. I was so sick at this time and could not get myself to work. June said that she would get me there and that I could ride with her every day if I needed to. It made sense, we would be living together and she could drive us that way I could get to work every day and not get discipline at work of my attendance problem. I said that would be wonderful. We finished packing and I moved in with she and her husband.

After I moved in with June and her husband I suffered from severe depression and I went into a trace like state in my mind. On the weekends I would stay in my room and read books from a library that I found near June's house. I lived my life in my head. I had along with everything else delusional thinking.

I thought about having a roommate and a pet pig that could do tricks. I began to eventually think that I had special powers and could communicate by sending brain messages to people and angels. I felt as if I were in a dream and could not wake up. I was stuck in my own little world.

I could not cope with life the way that it was for me. I began to sleep all day and all weekend and only left my room for work, water and to go to the bathroom. June tried to get me out of the house but I just wanted to sleep.

At work I listened to a head set with my cassette radio and had severe delusional thinking. I thought about at times how I wished I thought like other people around me and could have a normal life. I just kept getting worse. I believe I had flash back hallucinations and was just a complete zombie.

When June and I would drive under a freeway ramp, I always thought the ramp would crumble in an earthquake and kill us. I was really paranoid and frightened and my thinking was out of reality.

I have had in the past a tooth pulled and I saw a dental postcard at work with a light around the tooth and I believed that was my tooth in heaven that was raptured and my tooth was waiting for me to come to heaven to retrieve it. All kinds of strange thoughts I was having and I couldn't get free from my thoughts. I could not think at all. I tried putting life together like a broken puzzle but I failed every time I tried.

Nothing made sense to me anymore. My brain was burned and I had to learn how to live with a mental illness.

During this time, I felt like I needed my family so I put in a transfer at work to go back to South Carolina. I eventually got the transfer and I changed my mind and stayed in California. It was the worst mistake I feel I ever made. I didn't know at the time that my life would get worse than it was, never imagined such a thing!

The Postal Service put me back on my night hours because I needed more documentation and I didn't provide it. I thought I could handle night work again so I didn't fight it. June's hours weren't mine anymore so we started driving by ourselves again.

Because I worked what we call tour one and June worked swing shift, tour three we didn't see one another very often. I slept all day before June went to work and she slept all night when I got home to her house.

June started acting strange and would wake me up so I could take a shower before she would go to work. I told her that I take my shower at night and that I didn't want to sleep on wet hair. She would get so upset and I could not understand why. She was acting strange.

One night I got home, June was sleeping on the sofa and I knew that she and her husband, Joe had been in a fight. She woke up when I went outside to smoke a cigarette and she said that maybe it was time for me to move out on my own. I had been there one year and a half. It was time for me to go.

Before I found an apartment, Joe was coming on to me in a sexual way. That was the last thing I needed in my life. Also, I wasn't attracted to him and the thought made me sick to my stomach. Joe would also leave roses in the shower before I would bathe and I felt very uncomfortable and knew that I needed to find a place to live immediately. I began looking and I would take just about anything that I found. While Joe and June's marriage was falling apart, I found an apartment in Long Beach not far from where I lived before with my roommate Paul. I took the apartment because it was near a lot of bars and I loved to drink and shoot pool.

When I began to move out of June's house, she accused me of having an affair with her husband, Joe. I told her that was a crazy thing to think and that I wasn't attracted to Joe. I also suggested marriage counseling to both of them but Joe would not take no for an answer.

That was just great. All I needed at the time was flash backs, a jealous wife and a husband who wouldn't leave me alone. I was very happy on my moving day. June helped me move a few things and I was once again, on my own.

Joe would come to my apartment once in a while to bring me flowers and a gift here and there. He found out where I lived by moving a few things for me in his truck. I didn't think he would go as far with me as he did.

Next time Joe came by, I had a black male neighbor yell at him and tell him to leave me alone or next time he would get it good. He left me alone after that.

While I lived in Long Beach, I would call in sick at work and I would go to the gay bars and dance and drink alcohol with the girls who went there. One night the black man, my neighbor, John was having a party with the drugs and the alcohol and I decided to go. I couldn't do the drugs because of my mental illness but I could drink and I did.

At this party I met a girl, Suzan and we became friends. I asked her if she would go out with me to a restaurant and she said that she would like to go. We made plans to go to the ship, the Queen Mary to have dinner. I would pay and she would go along, looking pretty.

We had a good time that night and she had a good time drinking wine and spending my money. Suzan was in college. She was thirty-five at the time and wanted someone to live with in a relationship. We talked about it a we began to look for a place to move in to, together.

We found a condo near the college she went to in Cerritos California. It was about twenty minutes from Long Beach and we liked it there. We rented the condo and I signed the lease. The condo was eight-hundred and fifty dollars a month and it was a three bedroom. I liked it and felt a little better at that time.

Suzan and I were in a relationship but she didn't want to have sex with me. She said that she wasn't very attractive to me and she liked someone else and just wanted to be roommates. I never had a problem before with my looks with other girls but I agreed to be just roommates with Suzan. She wanted my money though and she did spend it.

Suzan and I would go once in a while to her mother's house. Her mother liked me and she was very nice to me. Suzan and she would fight all of the time, so it wasn't to nice going over there. I stayed with Suzan's grandmother once and I talked with her about Suzan not giving me any rent money. Her grandmother told me that Suzan must be paying me something and I told her that she wasn't paying me one penny of the rent.

It was hard on me paying all of the bills. I finally told Suzan that she would have to move out because I wanted a relationship with someone and we weren't in one so, I wanted out of the living arrangement. I told her that there was a good college in Palm Springs, California and that she should consider moving there. I also told her that Palm Springs has very hot weather and that she liked hot weather.

Palm Springs is about two hours away and I wanted to get Suzan as far away as I could from me. Suzan was also very mean to me at times. I had all I could take from her. I told her that she could stay for a couple of more months and then she would have to move out.

Her mother found her an apartment in Palm Springs and a friend helped her move out. That was a nice break and with my mental illness, I felt I could get some rest and be alone for a while.

I met a woman named Kathy and she was older than me. I was thirty-two and she was forty years old. I met her at a New Years Eve party and we got into a relationship together.

After about four years I began to listen to a Pastor on the radio and really loved his teaching. It felt good trying to seek the Lord, Jesus again. I also began going to church at a Calvary Chapel and felt like I was in the wrong kind of relationship, so I ended the sexual relationship with Kathy.

We became friends instead and that seemed to work out very well. We always had a good time together and I really enjoyed our friendship very much. She was very patient with me having a mental illness and I became delusional often. It was a hard time in my life but I had to make it work. I continued going to church and I began to change in my heart toward God.

I thought that maybe God could help me with my life and my mental illness. I feel now that God allowed me to suffer for growth in my life. I couldn't understand why I had to suffer such mental anguish. It was horrible and I was in and out of hospitals at times while living in Cerritos.

My and Kathy's friendship did end. We had several fights one in which I was very sick and she was busy at work and would not give me a ride to the hospital. I really needed to go to the hospital because I was hallucinating and very delusional. The medication my doctor had changed to Depakote and it was for mania and depression. I kept getting sick on Depakote and needed to find something else to take.

I had built up my savings account and I'm glad I did. I was very depressed with clinical depression and was once again, in the hospital. The hospital had me on Depakote and an antipsychotic medication. I remember staying in my room, asleep and I could not wake up. The hospital staff would check on me once in a while, but I stayed in bed for two weeks.

While I was in my room, I believed that I was in a tomb and waiting for Jesus to raise me from the dead. I was happy to be sleeping because I was suffering also with severe mania. My mind was racing really fast before I was admitted to the hospital. That is one of the reasons I went into the hospital. Depression and mania. It was a terrifying experience for me.

When I was released from the hospital, I went into a deep depression and was out of work on medical leave. I slept about eighteen hours a day for one year and only got up for the bathroom and to eat. I lived off of my savings account for that year. It was a hard thing to go through.

I would not even shower at all. Taking a shower felt like I had run around the block five times. I was exhausted and afraid that things would never get better.

I began to see a Christian therapist, Doctor Browning. He cost one-hundred and fifty dollars an hour but I didn't care. I needed help in my life and was desperate to get help.

We talked about God's hand in my life and how to trust Jesus Christ. I had a hard time with trusting God. I felt like I had been through so much and wasn't getting any better. I wanted so bad to serve God but I didn't know how or where to begin. I was going to church but I needed a role model to learn from so I began to look for a friend at church.

I felt like I needed a friend who understood a little about some of the things I have gone through and a loving person. I had tried to make friends with others but always felt out of place and like I didn't fit into the crowd. My mind wasn't like other people's minds. I never thought in reality. Most of the time I had some delusional thinking and no one understood me when I would try to talk to others about my thoughts.

I didn't have any friends and wanted so bad to be accepted by others. I thought that one day I would find someone to talk to about anything and I found out later in life that, that friend was Jesus. I needed him so desperately and believed that he didn't love me. I thought for sure I was rejected and that I was going to hell. I knew that I had walked away from him because I was so angry at God but I also knew God was the only one who could put my life back together again, if it was ever together.

I didn't know how to live or how to take care of myself. I could never get well from the horrible things that had happened to me. I thought to myself, how could I ever serve God or even change. Later I realized that God wasn't asking me to change, he loved me for who I am.

There were some people in the church who had a different opinion than that and they let me know about it. There were some people in the church who loved and cared about me but they didn't make time for me in their lives. Everyone is always to busy to care for others who are hurting unless these people are in some kind of ministry. I really needed love from others and didn't know how to ask for help.

I needed support and realized that I was too mentally crushed to befriend these people.

Who wants to be friends with someone who is mentally ill? Maybe another mentally ill person? You never know what you will get on the next turn and after the friendships that I did find later, I would have been better off being alone.

CHAPTER

8

I was sitting at a table in the coffee shop at the church and a girl asked if she could sit down with me. I told her yes and she began to tell me that she was Bi-Polar. I thought to myself, finally, someone who could understand what I was going through. She was bleached blond and was forty-five. I was forty-one at this time and I was having a hard time financially.

I began telling her about myself and told her at times, I couldn't make it to work because I was so sick all of the time. After talking some more she said that she was renting a room at a half way house and was looking for another place. I told her that I was looking for a roommate and we talked about her coming to live with me.

We agreed that she should come over to see my place on a Tuesday and we exchanged phone numbers. We finished drinking our coffee and I told her that I had to go early and get to bed because I wasn't feeling well with my depression. We said good-bye and I waited for her to call and confirm our meeting one another at my place.

She did come over to the condo I was renting in Cerritos and liked her room. I had a three-bedroom condo I was renting and the rent was now one-thousand dollars a month. It was low for three bedrooms but the owner liked me. If I could go to work, I could have afforded it and wouldn't need a roommate. She decided that she wanted to move in the following week.

I did some cleaning and we had lunch a few times. We seemed to get along fairly well and soon became good friends along with being roommates.

After we were living together about three months, I found out that she was very delusional and believed that she was a prophet from God. She began telling me things that God was saying to her and I thought everything was a little weird. She prayed a lot and would tell me that she thought I was an immature Christian and that I was in darkness.

She went to prophetic churches and I would go with her at times. At these churches people were falling down on the floor when they had hands placed on them and I thought at the time it was really cool. We went a few times to Los Angeles for prophetic meetings and I began missing church at Calvary Chapel which is where I went to church.

Doing this for some time I began feeling very sick and delusion and began missing work again. I just didn't feel right and began getting really depressed. My roommate said that she was going to a counselor at Calvary Chapel. She suggested I see her and that talking to her might help me a great deal. I made an appointment and went to see her.

When I went to see the church counselor, I told her that I used to be in gay relationships and she was surprised. I told her that I was no longer in these relationships and that I also suffered from depression and at times delusional thinking and hallucinating. She gave me bible verses to read and told me to see her the following week. I made the appointment.

Talking to my roommate for some time, she found out that I used to be gay. She began telling me I was a sinner and she started treating me a lot differently. My roommate would have sessions with the church counselor and then she would come home and tell me what they talked about. They were slandering me and gossiping about me. I was really hurt that she, being a church counselor, would do such a thing to me. My roommate began telling me that she felt very uncomfortable around me and that the counselor told her not to walk around in her underwear around me. My roommate began telling her that I was looking at her and coming on to her in a sexual way. I told them both that they didn't know what they were talking about.

This was never a problem until she and my roommate learned about my past. Talk about judging another person! I was really hurt by this and cried a lot about it. I made an appointment with her again and the church told me that she would not see me anymore. I was devastated and it hurt so bad. I was crying and felt crushed inside of myself.

The church mentioned another counselor and said that she would be glad to see me so I eventually went to see her.

My roommate began making arrangements to move out and I was glad that she was leaving. Nothing but judgment from her and I felt very uncomfortable around her myself. I was sad that I was losing a friendship but her leaving was the best thing for me. She finally did move and once again I lived alone in my depression.

I made an appointment to see the church counselor and when I went to see her, I really liked her. She was defiantly a Christian and Jesus meant every thing to her and she followed the bible and lived the life of a saved, baptized in the Holy Spirit Christian.

She began telling me that her son was gay and that this really upset her. She told me that she keeps him and prayer but she couldn't find him and didn't know where he was. She had called his roommate and lost touch with her son. This was really bothering her and I could tell.

We began talking about Jesus and the things of the bible. She told me that Jesus had to be first in my heart. She also told me that I needed to love him supremely because of what he had done for me on the cross. I wanted to put this into practice and began going to church faithfully. I loved going to church and I felt happy to be serving God.

I tried to read my bible but I didn't at the time feel very connected to God. I did not know what was wrong but after going to church for a while, I felt a little bit better when I read my bible and felt I was growing some.

I was once all alone and there weren't many people at church to connect with for a friendship. I wanted so bad to have friends who didn't take from me so much. There are some things that I didn't like about church and that was one of them. I continued to go to church though and really liked it there.

Later some things would transpire that would make me feel differently though and that, I will never forget.

I had a psychiatrist who was also in Cerritos near where I lived. I was seeing him once a month for medications for my drug side effects. He seemed to be a nice doctor and I liked seeing him. He took a lot of time with me, asking me questions about myself which for me, was different than the other doctors I had seen in my past. I didn't know that he was going on vacation and would be out of town with no back up doctor to take his place while he was gone.

As I was at work one night, I began to get very delusional and knew that I had to refill my medication soon. I needed my medication or I would get very sick. I was taking less medication to stretch it out some in case I did run out. I decided I needed to call my doctor for refills. I found out that he was out of town and I asked if there was someone else to fill my prescriptions. I was told that there was no one to do it and that I would have to wait until he got back to the office.

I asked when would he return and I was told in three weeks. I told the secretary that I needed my medication right away and I asked if she could call him. I was told that no she couldn't call him. I knew that I needed to do something or I would be back in the hospital again.

I called my medical doctor, primary. He told me later over the phone that he couldn't find my file and that I would have to go to another doctor for prescriptions. I told him that I couldn't get in to see anyone else and he told me that he could not help me at that time.

I was fighting with delusional thinking and I was hallucinating some. I called my pharmacist and asked them if they could refill and I was told no once again. I did not know what to do and my television set began turning the pictures into cartoons. I knew I was sick but I could not control the situation at all. I was out of work by this time and could not function very well in my thinking.

Soon I was low on money and I would just throw my bills onto the coffee table in my living room and I would try to keep my head together and figure out what to do. I thought I could get a loan from work and eventually I forgot about all of my money and bills and became very sick. I would just sit at home and listen to music while hallucinating and being very delusional in my mind.

I called a Christian therapist that I knew and asked for prayer and also, I asked when he would be available for a phone call. His secretary set me up a time to call him, so I did. When we talked on the phone, I told him that I was very sick and I needed a lot of prayer. He told me that he had the name and phone number of a doctor that I could call and gave me the information. I hung up the phone and did call this doctor and left a message for him.

I told him on his recorder that I was very sick and needed an appointment right away. I waited for him to call me. The doctor did return my call two days later. By this time, I was really sick and didn't live in reality anymore. It was hard to think and I almost forgot my name.

The doctor told me that I needed to come in and see him before he prescribed medication for me. I made the appointment for that coming Monday. I told him about my symptoms and he began telling me about the medication that he would like to try with me. I listened and anything was better than my Depakote that I was on. I told the doctor that I kept getting sick on it. I hung up the phone and began to wonder why I had to go through all of this. I felt it would be better to die than live like this. I thought I would never get my mind back after this episode. I tried to sleep that night but my mind was racing so bad that I could not rest. I smoked a lot and tried really hard to stop thinking delusional thoughts. I was still hallucinating but not as bad as before.

Monday came and I had been awake for three days. I had a hard time driving but made it to my doctor's office. His office was in Anaheim and it took about half an hour to get there. I waited in the waiting area and tried to fill out paper work that was required. Finally, he called me back to his office and began talking to me.

He recommended Lamictal and Geodon medication. The Lamictal was for mania and depression and the Geodon was for psychosis. I told him that I would try it and that anything was better than Depakote medication. He wrote me a prescription and I left his office and went right to the pharmacy. The pharmacist told me that they could not fill the prescription that day and that I would have to wait a day.

I said that I was sick and needed the medication right away. Finally, they said that they would fill the prescription but that I would have to wait about an hour. I waited and then went home with my medication.

I knew that night when I took my medication that I needed to get back to work as soon as possible but I could no longer think properly to do my job. I didn't know what to tell work so I asked my doctor later to fill out paper work saying that I had anxiety and he did agree to do it for me.

After a few days I still wasn't getting very much better and called my psychiatrist. The doctor said that the medication would not start working right away and that I would have to wait about one or two weeks to get the full effect. I wanted to cry and I was so upset. I thought I would get better right away. I just had to wait.

I had very little money and could only buy very little food to eat. I filled out paper work to get a twelve-thousand-dollar loan from work and knew that the money would take time to get to me. I had a few days of sick leave at work but it wasn't enough money to pay my bills. I began missing my rent payments and called the owner of the condo, Jerry and explained the situation to him.

I told him that I would pay him back rent as soon as I got my loan from work and thank God, he agreed. After about two weeks I was feeling better and was able to go back to work. I will never forget that trial and it defiantly was one. I thought that my mind would explode I was so sick! I began hating Willy for what he had done to me and I was very sad about it.

I never imagined that someone would do such a horrible thing to me and destroy my mind. I had brain damage from the LSD that Willy drugged me with and would have to live like this for the rest of my life, I thought. I am so hurt by this betrayal and I try not to think very much about it but it is always with me.

The Lord has helped me to forgive.

I decided that it was time for me to get back to work so I went in on a Tuesday night. We had a Supervisor there who did not like me at all. He was giving me a hard time about not being at work. This time

I was gone a month and a half. I told him that I mailed my papers in and that I should be excused. He was still giving me a hard time and I told him I would go to the Union if he didn't leave me alone.

I felt exhausted and didn't feel like fighting with anyone. This Supervisor was making things really difficult for me at work. I felt like I was going to have a nervous breakdown. He would come up to me and tell me that I wasn't working fast enough and I couldn't move any faster without hurting myself.

I did eventually get hurt. I hurt my arms really bad and worked anyway. I told him that I was hurting but he didn't leave me alone and wanted more productivity from me. I was working as hard as I could but nothing was good enough for him.

One night I went to the bathroom and when I got back to my machine this Supervisor was there and pulled me off of the machine and told me I was hurting his productivity and that I needed to stay on my machine.

I decided to file a grievance with the Union. I did file and won the grievance. I was told I could go to the bathroom whenever I needed to without permission. I was happy about that and went when I needed to go instead of holding it. This made the Supervisor really angry so, he started harassing me in other ways.

He told me that working slow, he could fire me and threatened to. I was so upset and I began calling into work sick just to stay away from him. To this day I have four hours of sick leave left because I used it all, twenty-five years' worth of sick leave. I have now been at the Postal Service thirty years and have never been treated so poorly.

He did eventually go somewhere else to work in the Postal Service but not at the Santa Ana Plant where I was. I wanted to celebrate as soon as I heard he had left and I was so happy. I found out though, that he has been watching my clock rings and attendance from another office, why I don't know. I'm just glad he is gone.

He told me once that he was a Christian, I just laughed!

I thank God that today is much better at the plant where I work. The Supervisors are almost all younger than me and they treat me with a little respect. That is very nice and makes things easier for me.

CHAPTER

I found that I was having a really hard time trying to quit smoking. I looked around for meetings for addictions and found a few that I didn't like very much. I saw at church a program listed for addictions groups on Tuesday nights. I was able to go to these meetings because my hours at work had changedSo, I found out what building the church was having these meetings and I made arrangements to go.

I could not stop smoking. I tried everything that I could think of. I would throw my cigarettes in the trash and then I would go through the trash trying to find them and when I did, I would smoke them all.

I hated myself for being a smoker and I hated myself even more because I could not stop killing myself. The thought scared me so I wanted to go to these meetings and see what the church could do to help me.

On Tuesday night of that week I did go and the group did a bible study and then would put chairs in a circle and go around the room and the people would talk to one another about the struggles they were having with their addiction. When they got to me, I told them that I was a smoker and needed help. For the first time I didn't hear that there were worse addictions than nicotine. I was surprised by that.

I went to the meetings for some time and never was able to stop. I think the stress in my life made me feel like I needed some kind of a drug to use to keep me calm. Every time I tried to quit smoking, I felt like I was going to have a nervous breakdown. My mind couldn't take it. I eventually turned to the nicotine lozenges and the gum. I was able to quit at that time using these two products.

With the lozenges I would at times get chest pains but I kept using them and then I became addicted to the lozenges. I was just exchanging one addiction to the other. The nicotine was too strong for me to let go of! I was stuck and didn't know how to get free. I continued to use the lozenges and just gave up on my addiction. I spent a great deal of money on my addiction to nicotine.

In these meetings I met a girl who was a recovering heroin addict and at the time I met her I didn't know that she had used heroin. We were talking in the group and she said that she was looking for a place to stay for she and her son and daughter but that she couldn't find anything for them because she couldn't afford it because she was on disability.

I told her that I had three rooms and if she wanted, she could rent the two. She was so excited and I was too. I had very little money and I was all alone and would love to have she and her children stay with me. She would only have her two children on the weekend when her ex-husband would bring the children by the condo to drop them off. She was fighting for custody and had to prove to a judge that she had a separated room for her son.

I asked her to pay me five-hundred dollars a month and she could do all of the cleaning and some of the cooking for us. She agreed and we both got along really well. She would move in on the next Saturday afternoon. She only had a few things and it wouldn't take her a long time to move. She had a male friend help her.

After she moved in, we went to church together a few times and then she stopped going. I was wondering why she stopped but I didn't really ask her or push her to go. Her children were staying with her ex-husband and they would stay with us on the weekends. She was fighting for custody and living with me was in her favor because her children had their own room.

In time as we were talking and I found out that she had another husband who just got out of prison for armed robbery. I also found out that they were both heroin addicts and he tried to rob a store to pay for his drugs. I was devastated and told her that he could not stay with us.

A Judge also told her that she could not have custody of her children because the kids could not be around her second husband. I didn't want him around but told her he could visit with us. She kept telling me that this guy was her husband and that he should be able to stay with us. I told her, No!

About three weeks after she moved in, I came home from church one morning and her husband that she was married to at that time, was in bed with her in her room. She introduced me and I said hello to him. In the evening that night, she wanted him to spend the night at the condo that we lived in and I told her no that he could not stay.

When I went to bed that night, she snuck him into her room and I didn't know it until I heard them having sex. I was very upset and felt like I wasn't being respected at all. I told her that if he were at the condo, that she would have to move out. My roommate said that she wasn't moving and that her husband should be able to stay and that he could come over anytime he wanted because she lived with me.

Her husband started hanging around and began staying. I kept telling them that I didn't want to live with a man and she kept trying to talk me into letting him stay. Every time I would come home from work at night, he was there spending the night with her. She kept asking if he could stay and I told her that he was staying over anyway, so I gave in and he moved into the condo with us.

Her children would stay with us on the weekend and I would remind her that the children were not supposed to be around her husband who was staying with us. She told me that it was none of my business, so I just let them do what they waned to do. I was tired of fighting with them about the issue and knew that the only way to get them out was to evict them.

Eventually they began stealing my money. Some how she got a hold of my bank cards and credit cards and began spending my money. I would get home from work and could tell that they had been in my room going through my things. I tried to tell them that they had to leave but they wouldn't go and told me to leave.

I was shocked by this because it was my home that they were living in. I didn't own the condo but I had rented it for twelve years.

My roommate began yelling at me about things and I begged God to get them out. I realized I had to leave because I believed it was something that Jesus wanted me to do. I, in the past, thought about moving but I had too many things and couldn't afford storage. I tried to sell everything but it didn't work out for me so I just stayed and the thought of moving left me.

I thought to myself that this situation was my chance to move so I began looking for a room to rent. It was a situation that I no longer felt safe. I believe that they began using drugs again and my roommate was yelling at me and threatening me a lot. I cried a lot of the time and having a mental illness didn't help things very much for me.

I found a couple of rooms for rent and made a decision to rent a room near work and church. I put down a deposit and would move into my new room on Saturday of that week. I came home and told my roommate and her husband that I was moving and they were devastated. I was paying all of the bills and rent and her husband was not working.

All he would do is play video games all week. I knew that they would be evicted and felt that it wasn't my problem or responsibility to take care of them. I could not wait to move. I would just take my clothing with me and I had to leave everything else.

I had a complete home of furniture, all things for the kitchen and other home things, twelve years' worth of belongings I would be leaving behind. I had no choice. I used my work loan, twelve-thousand dollars for bills and back rent. I could not afford my own place at that time. I asked my neighbor if she wanted any of my things and told her a little about the situation at home and that I was moving.

My neighbor came over and I showed her all of my things and told her that she could have anything that she wanted. I told her I would be getting a hotel room on Friday night and I would come for my things on Saturday. She said that on Friday she would bring some men over to get my things that I was giving her. I was grateful that she would be taking some of my things and I didn't want my roommate and her husband to get all of my things.

On Friday of that week, before I went to work, I packed a bag with a few of my things. My blow dryer, some shampoo and some socks and underwear. I knew that I would be getting a hotel room after work at about one o'clock in the morning and I needed these things after I would wake up. I would take a shower in the morning before coming to the condo to get my things on Saturday.

Just before I left, I looked around at my home and my things. I realized that I would be leaving everything behind and I felt like my life was falling apart. I was really sad but told myself that I could start over with a new life and learn something about true friendship with others in the future.

After I got off of work, I finally found a hotel room. I had gone to a few places and they didn't have any rooms available there. I got a key to open the door and went inside and fell onto the bed. I was really tired and emotionally torn apart inside. I wondered why my life had been so bad and prayed a lot. I felt all alone and didn't know what would happen in the morning. I was able, eventually, to fall asleep.

In the morning, on Saturday, I called my neighbor and told her that I would be coming by the condo to get my things and told her that I appreciate her offering to help me get some of my things and to help me move. She told me that it wasn't her problem and that I would have to do it myself. I was shocked! I had given her everything that belonged to me that she wanted except the things in my room. I thought to myself how could she be so mean and cold towards me? I just didn't understand and told her that I must have been mistaken and thought she said that she would help me.

She then said that she would help me and I thanked her. I hung up the phone and got into my truck and drove out to the condo. I was able to get a hotel room in Cerritos so the condo wasn't far.

When I got there, my roommate's car wasn't there. She and her husband were not there. I got my keys out of my pocket and put the key into the door lock and my key would not turn. I tried a few more times and realized that my roommate and her husband changed the locks. I was devastated! I could not believe that they did that to me!

I tried to call a lock smith and could not reach anyone on my cell phone. My neighbor brought me a hammer and told me to break the windows. I did not want to do that but I had no other way to get into the condo. I wrapped the outside rug on the patio around my hand and arm and took the hammer in my hand. I hit the storm window a few times and then the glass broke and fell to the ground. I jumped back so the glass would not cut me.

After the window was broken, I reached my hand in and unlocked the front door. I walked into the living room and looked around. My neighbor took a few things but also left a lot of things there. I could not take any of it because my room that I would be renting was a small room. I only had enough room for my things in my room.

I walked into my room and nothing was there. All of my things were gone except a small television set and a video recorder. I looked onto the floor and there was a sleeping bag left for me. I opened my closet and everything had been taken. All of my clothes and shoes. Jewelry and other things were taken from me. My neighbor told me that all she had for me was a small bag of clothes and my wire to charge my cell phone.

I had a lot of nice things that were taken from me. I couldn't believe any of it. The whole situation was a night mare and I wanted to cry. It was horrible!

I packed my truck with the television set, VCR and sleeping bag. I also had a box of receipts that I took with me. It would not be much help because they were already stealing my money. I would have to start over with new account numbers and pin numbers for my banking. I waved good-bye to my neighbor and drove off. I drove down the freeway preparing to start over with a new life and the thought made me feel a whole lot better inside.

It began to rain and I thought that it was a perfect day for the rain. All of my things getting soaked with water in the back of my truck.

What a way to end my day. When I made it to my new place, the lady that I moved in with, Deborah, was sleeping so I tried to be as quiet as I could. I walked to and from the front door of her house with the few things I had and when I opened the bag of clothes that the neighbor gave me, I had two pair of slacks and two shirts and the clothes on my back.

Talk about starting over. I would have to shop for clothing the next day on Sunday. I had no underwear or no socks. I would go to the stores the next day and try and replace some of my personal belongings.

I decided to go to bed early and try and to forget about the things that had happened. I had my medication in my bag, in my truck so I took the medication and went to sleep. Hours later my cell phone rang at three o'clock in the morning and it was my roommate. She said that I broke into her house. I could not believe it! Her house? I just had to laugh and say, I broke into my house then I hung up the phone.

At that point I looked up out of the window into the dark and fear hit me. I realized that Satan lived in their hearts and they really believed his delusional lie that my home was theirs. I was fearful for them. I knew that God would not let them get away with what they had done to me. I lay on my sleeping bag and tried to tell myself that I could start over and that God would help me get through my emotional turmoil and restore my life. I feel asleep after a few more hours and would change my phone number that week.

Sunday morning, I took a shower and went to Church. I saw a friend and told her that the clothes on my back and a few others was all I had. She was shocked but told me that God was going to help me put things back together in my life. I felt sick and hoped I wouldn't get delusional again. I tried to forget everything and when I got home, I began to read my Bible.

I read my Bible day and night. I lay on my sleeping bag every day and would just read my Bible. In time my mind began to heal some. I wasn't getting sick anymore. I felt like the Bible verses were all that I was thinking about in my mind and I felt better inside. I thought that maybe to heal was possible after all.

As time went on, I enrolled in Bible College and began taking classes in the mornings. I worked at the Postal Service from four pm until twelve thirty am and had time for school in the mornings. I also began serving at the church and was answering phones in the mornings and was also working with the young school children.

The church that I began serving in, was right across the street from where I lived in Costa Mesa. I was in Santa Ana but right across the street, Costa Mesa began. I loved that church and the Bible College was also part of that church, Calvary Chapel. I wanted to be a part of ministry there at that church and began getting involved in all kinds of things there.

I was feeling better and was very happy at that time. I felt that things were getting better in my life and I looked forward to what my future may become.

CHAPTER

10

One evening on a Sunday night I went to a bible study at the church and met a man there named Ken. I found out that he was part of a Security Team and I told him that I was interested in security. He introduced me to a man named, Jim, who was head of the security team and Jim told me to attend a meeting the following Sunday after church. I said that I would and I was very excited about it.

I did attend the meeting and Jim was teaching things about keeping safety in the church and looking after the Pastor. The Pastor of the church, Pastor Chuck was very well known around the world and received a lot of threats from people because he spoke truth and offended a lot of people all of the time. Jim taught us how to take guns away from people and how to defend the people who attended the church.

I was so excited and the guys were really nice to me. I and one other girl were on the team but the rest were men. I would be serving on the team that night and I thought I would really enjoy serving God and the church in this position.

That night I walked to church and got there a six pm. I waited outside of the sanctuary until I was let inside. The security team met in a prayer room near the sanctuary and while meeting, I was given my first position. I would work outside that night and keep and eye on the fellowship hall. The fellowship hall had a big screen where some people would meet to watch the service. It gave people the opportunity to walk around outside if they wanted to.

At this time in my life, I was feeling very well medically and wasn't getting sick anymore. I was reading the bible a lot and it was, I feel, renewing my mind. The scriptures I was reading was staying in my mind and I would think about them a lot of the time. I felt that my mind would heal, after all.

That night I walked over to the fellowship hall and there was a young girl about seventeen outside putting her hands on the walls and looking up into the sky. She was also wearing a music headset without a radio. I asked her if everything was alright and she just mumbled to me. Just then her father came outside and told me that she had mental problems and a mental break down. I asked him if she was on medication and he said that she was.

I asked him what kind of medication that she was on and he told me what it was, I don't remember. I asked him if she ever tried Lamictal and Geodon and he said that she has not tried it or been on it. I told the girl's father that I have had a lot of success with the two medications. He was very interested in what I was saying to him. We continued talking and one of the guys on the team walked over and asked me if I was alright. I told him yes and he kept walking. Mark, the security team leader kept walking by to see if everything was okay. I kept telling him that everything was fine.

As I was talking to the girl's father, his daughter said that the fellowship hall was loud with the speakers and that she couldn't go inside. I told her that everything was going to be alright and I wrote my medications down on a piece of paper for him. I told him that Lamictal was for mania and depression and that Geodon was for psychosis. He thanked me and the service was ending so I said good night to them and walked off. I felt really good that I could help someone that night. I was hoping that the girl would be okay and believed that if her father asked her doctor for the medication that I recommended, she would get better, at least some what better. I met with the guys to turn in my radio and ear piece and they asked me if everything was alright earlier and I told them that it was. I also told them that I was just talking to these people.

I walked home that night late and was very happy with my life and how it had been turning out. I was smiling, for a change. In the morning I would be serving at an office at the church before I would go to work.

In the morning I got up and drove my truck to the church. There was a building near the church, the same building that the college was in, and I started my day at a desk. I was also putting together class papers for the children that school year.

I worked for the Hands of Hope ministry and the ministry had a Release Time Christian Education for young children in the public schools. The children had a permission slip for their parents to sign and the children would come to a bus and trailers to study and be taught the bible.

The children would study during their lunch hour and we would go and get their lunches for them. I felt that the ministry was wonderful but I was shocked that the public schools would not let us use their facilities. We could use the restroom but that was all.

I was one of the drivers and felt privileged that the church would allow me to drive one of their buses. It was fun serving there. I also answered phones in the office. I made a lot of friends at the church and these ministries at this time in my life. I really loved what I did there.

I would get there at ten am and stay until four in the afternoon. I would either drive to work or walk. I could walk to work because my job was right next door to the church. I would get to work early and talk to people about what I was doing at the church. I was so happy and I didn't get very sick because I was reading my bible and my head was filled with good things from the New Testament.

On Sunday mornings and nights, I would serve on the security ministry. The church had three services and I would go to the second and third service to serve there. I would always smoke a cigarette before church and then spray myself with air freshener that I kept in my truck. I always worried that the guys would smell smoke on me but no one ever said anything to me about it.

Before service would start, we would all meet in the prayer room to get our radios and assignments. I would be outside a lot and really liked it very much. I would talk to a lot of people and made a lot of friends. A lot of the guys would talk with me about their marriages and children. Some of them had bad marriages and would ask me questions about things pertaining to women.

I couldn't offer too much advice because I didn't understand relationships on their level. I would just listen most of the time and that was really all I could do.

There was a guy there at church on the team that I really liked. It was my second male attraction in my whole life. The other attraction was a pastor at the college and I was really attracted to him too.

The guy at church was a former Marine and he had the personality of a service man. Very clean hair cut and very quiet at times. He knew I liked him but because he had problems with his ex-wife, he treated me poorly. I liked him so much, I didn't care how he treated me. I tried to talk with him some but he was quiet most of the time. I kept trying though.

He met a woman there at church and wanted to marry her. He eventually did and I was very hurt but told myself that he treated me bad so if I had a relationship with him, it would have never worked out. I just kept quiet about how I felt and moved on into other interests.

After I would walk the church grounds, all of it, a new pastor took over the ministry and he got us carts to use. They were like golf carts and had electric motors. I loved driving these carts and would give people rides to the front of the church at times. I would talk with women in my cart who were crying and telling me personal things about their lives. I felt sorry for them and told them that I would pray for them. I loved my job at the church.

Eventually I was put back stage to watch the security camera. One of the guys on the team wanted a girl friend so we would scan the camera all over the sanctuary and look at all of the girls that we thought were beautiful. I saw a lot of things on the camera like people bringing drinks in the sanctuary, which weren't allowed and I saw people standing up and yelling at the pastor at times.

When people would stand up and shout, it was our job to walk them out. Sometimes it would turn into a violent fight and we would have to call the police. Some of the guys on the team were police officers and that helped a lot at times.I only had three problems in security the rest of the time, the guys handled everything else. It was scary at times but I got used to it.

After third service I would drive home and then walk to church at six pm, Sunday nights. A girl renting a room in the same house I was in, was a missionary and we talked some about the bible. She would walk to church with me and we would wave good-bye and I would go to the prayer room for my night assignments.

Most of the time, I was outside at night. I could hear the loud speakers and I would listen to the service and the music. Sometimes I would walk far and would miss some of the service but for the most part, I heard it. I could also hear all of the activity going on at the church on my radio. I would sometimes take the ear piece out of my ear when I would sit inside, just to hear the service. It was all good and I felt like I was part of something. At last my life seemed like it was getting better for me, I was happy at that time.

The guys never knew about myself and the things that have went on in my life. I never wanted to tell anyone that I have had female relationships in my life or that I was mentally ill. I was ashamed of all of it and didn't want anyone to know. The girl that I lived with, the missionary, told some people about my illness. No one ever mentioned it except once and I didn't deny it. I just told them I was okay now and not to worry about it, it was my problem.

Back at home I would walk to the store every day and buy cigarettes. I smoked a lot and was ashamed of it. The lady who owned the house could smell the smoke on my clothes and would always say something about it. I wanted to quit smoking but I could not stop. I tried everything! I was so afraid of getting lung cancer and I prayed to be okay physically. It was something that had a hold of me and I felt I could not do anything about it.

I bought some nicotine lozenges and began using those. It began to work very well for me and I liked them. I was getting enough nicotine in my body and I felt like I had smoked. I then stopped buying cigarettes and spent a fortune on the lozenges. The lozenges cost a lot more than cigarettes and I felt that was bad. People want to quit smoking but the cigarette companies make it hard by charging so much.

A trip to the hospital would cause me to start smoking again. This time it would be a really bad situation!

At the camera during church services, in the mornings, I would put lozenges in my mouth. Almost the whole pack of lozenges and I would feel very sick. Eventually, my mouth would begin to bleed and I would have blisters all over my gums. It was horrible, but like the cigarettes, I was addicted and could not stop. I just continued using them and my mouth kept bleeding, but I liked the way that they made me feel.

I would use them at work, at the Post Office too and would throw up in big trash cans that we had on the machines. I would pack a lunch so I wouldn't gag without food being in my stomach. I would have something to vomit and I would feel better.

I almost went back to cigarettes at this time but wanted to stay off of them because it took me so long to quit. At church and at the hands of hope ministries, I would go outside in my truck and suck on lozenges and listen to music. I felt like it was my new drug. It made me feel better when I was under a lot of stress. With my mouth bleeding so bad, I would chew the nicotine gum sometimes and it was alright but I preferred the lozenges.

I spent a great deal of money on these stop smoking products but they never really took away the craving for cigarettes. I felt terrible using all of these things because I was a Christian and wanted to be free from any addiction. I went for prayer a lot for the nicotine use and I probably would have been able to stop but I started smoking when I was nine-years-old and I didn't know how to live without nicotine. I just continued to use these products and I believe nicotine will numb the pain in my life from my past.

I began having a really hard time sleeping so my doctor prescribed Ambien for me in order to sleep so I wouldn't have any mania episodes. When I began taking Ambien, I would sleep very well but then I began sleep walking and also driving in my sleep. I would drive to the store and buy food and when I would wake up, I could not remember driving anywhere to get the food.

Later on, I still couldn't sleep so the doctor told me that I could take Ambien until it started to work. I don't know why he told me that but I began taking seven to nine Ambien a day. I could fill them anytime I wanted because my medical insurance did not cover them and they weren't that expensive so I would pay cash for them out of pocket.

I would turn my prescriptions in to different pharmacies so I could fill several prescriptions at the same time. I was taking so many a day and my doctor just kept writing prescriptions for me.

One afternoon I was trying to sleep after serving at the church and I took about seven Ambien, three Temazepam-for sleep, four Benadryl and three Tylenol aspirins. When I lay down on my sleeping bag, I thought I might die but I didn't care. I had so many drugs in me, I wasn't thinking clearly. I did finally fall asleep and woke up later that night. I missed going to work and would have to call in sick to cover myself, so I did.

The next morning when I went to the church, to serve at hands of hope, I was so sick and my face was swelling really bad. I just began drinking coffee and tried to keep myself together. I still continued taking a lot of Ambien because I couldn't sleep. It was a crazy time in my life and I don't know why I had insomnia but I did. I would do anything to sleep and felt I was going to go crazy. I missed a lot of work and wanted to always sleep as much as I could.

I still served at the church in security and at hands of hope even when I would call into work sick. I loved my job at the church and didn't want my insomnia to interfere with my positions there.

I stayed up all night and just read my bible. Sometimes I would sleep after reading but not always. I tried anything to sleep. After hours of being awake, I would sleep getting a few hours in. It was hard to live like this but I managed to live as close to a normal life as I could. I didn't tell anyone what was happening and felt a lot of stress. I was afraid if I didn't sleep, I would get sick again. At this time, I never did but things would change later.

I was told that lack of sleep could cause someone to become manic in their behavior and start to think delusional thoughts. I was so afraid and didn't want to relive the things that I had in the past. I just stayed plugged into church and serving. I tried to go to work but I missed a lot of days because of my insomnia.

I had a doctor write on medical papers that I had insomnia and that excused me form working every few days. I liked staying home anyway but my money was slowly disappearing so I needed to work. I would go into work sick from all of the medication I was taking. I was able to make it through but it took a lot of time before I could sleep good again. Eventually, I was able to sleep some but not very long at one time. I would sleep a few hours at a time but it seemed to work for me.

I was still up all hours at night and something good happened at the Post Office, they abolished my job and I would be working nights from ten pm until six-thirty am. It would work for me I thought. The only thing that bothered me was, they were moving me to a new facility at a smaller building about fifteen miles from home. I had to stop serving at hands of hope.

CHAPTER

11

My job at the Post Office was now at a small plant in Santa Ana. My hours had changed to night hours and I was able to serve still in the security ministry at church. I couldn't serve at night but only morning services. I was able to sleep during the day a little better than before because I was so tired from my job at the Post Office. We ran double the mail on the machines than I was used to running. It was very hard work.

The first night I began working there, I met a guy I have seen at the plant named, Victor. He was a Hispanic male and he was very kind to me. He was at the, North Grand facility, that's what the building was called, for three years and he began showing me around. We both got to work very early so we had time to walk around and I could see the building I was working in.

We became good friends and every night we would get to work very early and sit and talk for hours. It didn't take me long to find out, through our conversations that he was a pervert and all he wanted to talk about was sexual things. I tolerated it because I didn't have friends outside of the church and I wanted a friend.

I tried talking to Victor about my faith but he didn't care anything about God or Jesus. He just talked about sex all of the time. I ignored the things he was talking about and at times would try to change the conversation.

Victor knew everything about sex you could imagine. I found out that he had a lot of pornography videos that he would lend out to the men at work. I personally don't think he had ever been with anyone sexually because he didn't take showers and he smelled pretty bad.

As we talked, in time, we decided to go to his apartment on a Saturday to watch a couple of movies and I thought it wouldn't hurt anything to go over to his place. We also talked about going to Disney Land and to me, that sounded like a lot of fun for me. I never had anyone at church or work who wanted to spend time with me doing things together. I asked him if the following Saturday would be good and he said that would be great.

He told me that he would call me to confirm and I told him that it would be fine to do that. I waited until that Saturday and wondered if it was the right thing to do. I thought about it and thought about it some more. I talked myself into going to his place and tried to tell myself that Victor would never do anything to hurt me. I had made my decision and I decided to go.

A couple of days before I went to Victor's apartment, a truck slammed into my truck and totaled it. I had to get a loan to buy a new car and I chose a second truck. We had to post pone until the following two weeks. I was so upset about the accident that I forgot all about my concerns about going over Victor's.

The weekend came where Victor and I got together at his place. He called me and said that he would meet me at work and that he would drive us to his place. I agreed and told him that I would walk to the Post Office near my home. He said that he would meet me there. I got dressed, blow dried my hair and began walking to the Post Office.

Victor was standing outside in the parking lot and welcomed me and then I got into his truck, we drove off. He said that he needed to get some ice at the liquor store and that he had pizza being delivered to his apartment later on that day. I said that it would be great and that I was hungry.

We stopped at the liquor store and Victor went inside. I sat in the truck and had strong conviction to get out of his truck and tell him that someone called me on my phone and I had an emergency of some kind and had to leave. I wanted to get out of the truck but talked myself, once again into going to his place. I tried to tell myself that he was my friend and would do nothing to me, I felt I could trust him and thought everything was just in my head.

Victor came back to the truck and got in. We drove off to his apartment. He lived close to me about twelve blocks away, I was surprised by that. When we went into his place, he put the ice in the kitchen sink and there were already sodas there. I opened a can and sat down in the living room. He got a box down from the top of the television set and pulled out a movie.

He started the movie and it was the worst one I had ever seen. The characters in the movie killed a couple and took on their identity and started to live like them, as them, the people they killed. It was a game they called it.

I would ask him some questions about the movie as we watched to try and keep my mind occupied with something other than what I was seeing.

After the movie, he let me pick and I picked a Russian sniper movie. He put the movie in and I really liked it. After watching it for a while, I excused myself to go to the bathroom. As I was coming back into the living room, I began to feel a little sick. I didn't know what was wrong. I sat down to watch the movie again.I picked up my soda can and took a few swallows of my drink and I began to get very delusional. I had no idea that he had drugged me because at that time I wasn't in my right mind.

I tried to watch the movie but the television was telling me things. I didn't know what to think. I would shake my head and try to concentrate. It wasn't working very well and like I said, I had no idea I had been drugged. My mind wasn't right and I couldn't think very well.

Then Victor grabbed me and tried to pull me in his direction. Eventually I was able to break his grip on my arm and I knew then that I was in danger. I knew I had to stay calm or I would be raped. I tried to act as if nothing was wrong and I kept watching the movie. I got sicker and sicker as the time went by.

Finally, the movie was over and I put my shoes back on and told him I was ready to leave and to take me home. Victor sat for a while and then he put his shoes on and we got in his truck and he drove me home. When I got home, I was so sick and delusional. I felt a strong sexual desire and still didn't know what was wrong. I took an Ambien and tried to relax some but I couldn't fall asleep. I just kept getting more delusional. It was horrible.

I was really scared and realized that the only friend that I had drugged me and I was a victim again. It really hurt me deeply and I didn't understand why God would allow these things to happen to me. I did know that God did love me and I would never believe differently. I knew that there were reasons as to why this had happened to me but at the time, I really didn't fully understand what they were. I knew I was in for another horrible trial in my life. I wished that I had listened to God when he was telling me in a strong way to get out of Victor's truck, and got out of it.

I sat in my room that night praying and asking God to help me sleep and to come down off of the drugs that Victor put in my sodas. I began taking some of my medication to try and change the way my brain was thinking. Nothing worked. I was awake night after night trying to think clearly and sleep and I could not.

I was so angry and about three days later, I called work and asked for time off and told my boss that Victor drugged me and tried to rape me. I didn't know if grabbing me was trying to rape me but, in my mind, it was. I wasn't in my right mind when I talked to my boss, I just knew I couldn't work because I was so doped up. My boss gave me the time off and she told me that I needed to go to the hospital and see a doctor and file a police report.

I told my boss, Terry that I thought I would be alright and that I just needed a few days rest. She told me it would be best to see a doctor. I told her I would if I got worse and thanked her for the time off and told her that I hoped to be doing better soon.

I sat in my room night after night getting more delusional and my thinking wasn't normal at all. After five days of being sick I began to think of crashing my truck. I was delusional and thought that one day I would die in a car accident and now was God's timing and crashing my truck was something he wanted me to do.

I didn't want to die but, in my mind, I thought that it was time to die.

I looked at myself in the mirror and decided that I didn't want to be found dead in my truck with what I was wearing so, I changed my shirt and made other arrangements for my death. I wrote a suicide not and put it on my little desk in my room and grabbed my keys and cell phone and started walking to my truck.

As I was walking to my truck, I decided I didn't want to die but it was time. I stopped and then began walking to my truck again and then I opened my phone and dialed, 911. The operator came onto the line and asked what was wrong and I told her that I thought I was going to hurt myself. I didn't know how to make the suicide thoughts go away and I was scared. I really believed that God wanted me to kill myself. I could not control the situation.

The operator told me to stay where I was and asked my address. I guess they didn't know because I was on a cell phone, so I gave her my address.

It seemed like seconds later, two police officers in two cars, pulled up very fast in front of the house and jumped out into my yard and asked what was wrong. I told them that I wanted to crash my truck and they said that they were glad that I called.

The officers asked my name and age and I told them, Chris, is my middle name that I go by and I was forty-six-years old. They asked if I had a mental illness and I told them, yes. I also told them that a guy drugged me and I became really sick and couldn't think clearly.

They asked about the situation but I couldn't tell them anything else because I was so sick and I couldn't think clearly. I mentioned God a few times and the police started talking to me about Jesus. They sat me down on my porch and asked me a lot of questions about my faith and the things that I believed. They then asked me to go and get my bible. I went inside and got my bible off of my desk. I then took my bible outside to them and they began reading it to me.

The police read verses to me and asked me how I was feeling and I told them I wanted to crash my truck. I then began asking them if I was dead and they told me that they were going to call a social worker over to check me out and see if I needed further assistance. They did call the social worker and she came over about half an hour later.

When she got to my house, they asked me if I had a gun or if I had taken to much of my medication. I told them, no I don't and I didn't take to much medication. She asked to see my room and asked where I kept my medication. I told her that I kept my medication in my dresser drawer. She asked to see it. I showed her my medication and she told the police that I needed to go to the hospital.

They police officers told me to volunteer to go to the hospital. I did agree with them because I wanted to commit suicide and was afraid that I would if I didn't go.

An ambulance came to the house and the paramedic strapped me to a gurney and put me into the back of the ambulance. Just then the police officer handed me my bible and they shut the doors. The ambulance began to drive off and, in a way, I was relived. I was hoping I would get some help at the hospital.

When I got to the hospital, the doctors and therapist began asking me a lot of questions. I told the doctor that I heard a voice that told me to kill myself. I felt they were evaluating me to see if I would hurt myself or anyone there. The doctors determined that I needed to be put in a suicide unit for two weeks and longer if necessary. They took me there and locked me into the unit and I thought for some reason that I was in Russia.

The only reason that I think, I thought that I was in Russia, is because I always wanted to go there on a mission trip with the church.

I finally saw a psychiatrist after I was in the hospital for about three hours. When I saw her, she asked how long had it been since I slept. I told her about three days, but it was longer than that. The doctor said that she would give me an injection that night to sleep. She said they had to get me to sleep or I wouldn't get better. I agreed and then I watched television the rest of the day. It was hard though because I was really delusional at that time.

I had forgotten to tell the doctor that I was drugged by a friend. They diagnosed me as being bipolar. I will later be diagnosed as being, Schizoaffective.

That night I was given a shot and I was relived because I am very sick and delusional when I can't sleep. It was a strong injection. I was asleep in seconds. When I woke up in the morning, I was very drowsy and had a hard time waking up. I took a shower and then went to the television room. later they allowed the patients to go outside to smoke a cigarette and I went with them and started smoking again.

When I got back to my room, my hat and bible were missing. They take things from your room in the suicide unit. I asked for everything back and they told me that I couldn't have both hat and bible so, I asked for my bible. I had a pair of glasses and wondered how long it would take them to realize that I could break them and slash my wrists with the glass. I kept my glasses and they never thought about it.

When I was admitted to the hospital, I called the church I attended and left a message for the Hands of Hope ministry. I needed to talk to the Pastor and I was afraid and lonely. To my surprise, the Pastor and a friend showed up at the hospital to talk with me. I told them that I was drugged and about the experience at Victor's apartment. They were upset about it and prayed for me that day. They gave me a lot of their support and I appreciated it very much.

The Pastor kept telling me that it wasn't my fault and not to blame myself. I remember asking God to forgive me if I got Victor into trouble at work. I felt bad about the whole thing, why, I don't know. The whole situation was horrible and I couldn't wait to get back home. I wasn't getting a salary but I had money in the bank at this time, thank goodness for that.

I was in the hospital for two weeks and then released. A taxi cab took me home and when I got there, I was so relieved to be in my room again. I just wanted to sleep and I was very tired. The doctors increased my medication but they did not change any of it. They gave me prescription strength Benadryl for sleep and that night I couldn't wait to get back to work in two days. I got a note from my doctor saying that I could return on a Monday night.

Monday night came and I left for work. When I got there, at North Grand, my supervisor, Dave said that I was supposed to be at the Plant that night, where I used to work. I told him that no one notified me of that and that my doctor said that I could return to work that night. Dave called his boss and he asked to speak to me. When I took the phone,he began yelling at me and gave me a direct order to go to the plant right then. I left there and was worried about the situation.

When I got to the plant, the MDO (Manager of District Offices) was there and a Postal Inspector, a man and they took me into a conference room and sat me down in there. They told me that it was against Postal regulations to call my boss and give a false report. I was told that after the interview that I would be either fired or suspended and that they would have to determine that after they ask me some questions. I told them the situation and that Victor drugged me.

It seemed that Victor told them that he was in a sexual relationship with me and that I was mentally ill and that is why I was in the hospital. They believed him and told me to sit there while they made a decision about whether I would be fired or suspended for lying.I was told I had given a false report and they suspended me until further notice. They took my badge and my time card and walked me out of the plant. I asked when I would be returning because I had bills to pay. The (MDO) said that he didn't know when I would be returning but that they would let me know.

When I left work, I stopped for gas and got a pack of cigarettes. I was shocked! I couldn't believe that I was drugged, suicidal, hospitalized and suspended from work all at the same time. When I got home, I had a hard time sleeping that night, it was awful! I decided right there and then I would put all of the situation that had happened into God's hands. There was nothing I could have done about it. I couldn't afford an Attorney and that was all I could think that might help me out. I just had to wait.

The next day I called my boss, and left her messages and I called the Union office and no one would return my calls. I kept calling every couple of weeks and I received no return calls or any information from anyone. I decided to let God give me my job back, so I did and I stopped calling them.

After one month, I received a letter in the mail from the Postal Inspection Service and they said that I was acting off duty unlike a Postal employee should be acting. Victor had told them that I took the drugs on my own and that he was just a victim of a mentally ill woman.

They also said that they wanted to know why I was in the hospital. I had already told them that I had been drugged but I didn't tell them that I was suicidal. I felt at this time that I needed to prepare for a new job, so I began looking. I haven't heard from the Union or my boss so I figured I would never go back to work.

About one month and a half later, I received another letter stating that I needed to seek new employment. I called my boss and I got ahold of her. She was asking for all kinds of documentation that I didn't have so she decided to send me to a Postal doctor so he could decide if I could come back to work or not. I waited for the letter to come in the mail and it never did.

I called the plant office and they said that I had an interview with the Postal doctor the next day. I thanked them and then got off of the phone. I could not believe all that I was going through. I also found out that the Postal Service moved all of the machines to the plant and all of the North Grand employees were going back to the plant. I was hoping that when or if I got my job back, they would move me alone but everyone was being moved.

I continued at this period of time serving in the security ministry and serving at Hands of Hope ministry at the church. I called a friend at church and told her all that was going on and she got me an Attorney, free of charge, who attended out church. I talked with him over the phone and he asked me if he could send a letter to my boss. I told him that it would be nice if he did that for me. He said that he would and if there were any thing else happening later on, to let him know about it.

The next day I went to the Postal doctor to be interviewed to find out if they would send me back to work. The Postal doctor asked me why I was in the hospital and he then asked what other reason was I there for. I told him that I became suicidal and needed to be admitted. He then asked me if I was mentally ill and I told him that the psychiatrist said that I was bipolar. The doctor then asked me about what happened a Victor's apartment and I told him he put drugs into my soda and that after drinking them I became delusional. He asked me a few more questions and then told me that I couldn't return to work because Victor worked there. I was shocked!

The Postal doctor said that he would need to talk to my psychiatrist and that she could call him that day on the next day.

When I left the Postal doctor's office, I was extremely angry and almost crashed my truck driving home. I was punching the steering wheel and screaming and cursing. My windows in my truck were rolled up and people could hear me screaming while we were sitting a stop lights waiting for them to turn green. In my entire life, I have NEVER been so ANGRY before. I never think that I will ever be that angry again. I could have killed someone that day.

I called my psychiatrist on my cell phone while driving and asked her to call the Postal doctor and to tell him that I was stable enough to go back to work. She said that she needed to see me first and asked me to make an appointment. I told her that I wanted to come to her office that day and she said that she had patients that she was seeing. I told her it would take a few minutes to call and she agreed to let me come to her office.

When I got to my psychiatrist's office, she saw me right away and after we talked, she called the Postal doctor. They talked for a few minutes and he told her that he would send a report into the Postal Service and that I would have to wait for the report to get there. After they hung up the phone, she hurried me out of her office and I thanked her on the way out.

I had to call my boss on several more occasions and she told me she would have to see the report before I could return to work. I was also told that my hours might change because they would have to ask Victor if I could still work the shift that he worked. Imagine that! I waited for about another two weeks, then my boss called and said that

I could return that night. The day of the week that she spoke to me on the phone.

Night came and I went back to work at the plant. When I got there, I was given a new badge and time card and I went to the area that I worked at before I went to North Grand. I clocked in and I was grabbed right away by a supervisor and put on a machine to work. Victor and all of the people who worked in North Grand were on the other side of the building so the MDO, left me in the area that I was in. That was a relief to me because I didn't have to see Victor any more.

I was very angry and upset about the whole situation. Victor's friends all laughed at me and made fun of me, calling me crazy. They told everyone that I had a mental illness and had a blast slandering me. It was awful. I will never forget it.

About one week after I returned to work, the (MDO) told Victor and I to stay in our own areas. He was on one side of the plant and I, the other. The only exception was on breaks in the cafeteria we could go to at the same time. I was alright with that and stayed in my area.

Victor on the other hand, would walk through my area, head held high like he was a king who won a war. He would look down my machine at me working just to harass me. I never went to Chuck or Terry about it. I figured his day would come and it did.

Victor was a diabetic and lost a leg and some toes. He was out of work and in a rehabilitation hospital after about three years from this incident. Later Victor died in his apartment and needless to say, I wasn't at his funeral. I remember praying for his salvation and hope he responded to God's call for his life.

The lady I lived with in Santa Ana, right next to my job and the church, was moving out of state for medical reasons. She had cancer and was going to be moving for treatment. She asked me to move out of her home. I told her that I would look for a place and I would leave as soon as possible. I started looking and found an add in the church office renters' book. I called a lady in Westminster, California and told her I was interested in the room. We made arrangements to meet at her place on a Tuesday of the following week. All of these things took place in 2012, I was forty-seven years old at the time.

On Tuesday of the following week, I met with this lady and decided I would take the room. I liked being there and would swim in the pool a lot. This lady lived in a condo and the people there were really nice. The lady I rented the room from, she and I would go to the movies together some of the time and church together. I still served on the security team and would let her back into the prayer room after services. I liked her.

She and her sister didn't get along very well and after witnessing a lot of family fighting, I decided to move out of her home. I found a studio room to rent in Garden Grove, California from a girl I knew at work. I decided to move into the room and was happy to get away from all of the arguing and fighting. The room was nice and I was upstairs on my own. The girl hardly ever bothered me and that was nice. Alone some of the time, at last. The Peace was nice. I felt then that I could recover from all that had happened to me. I continued going to the same church and really loved my life again.

I took some time but I slowly began to forget about all that had happened to me. Things at work were getting better and I was making new friends. I was put in another area at work and my hours would eventually be changed for a short period of time. I was still working at night but the hours were from one o'clock am to ten am. It worked for me. I could spend all three services at the church I was attending and get enough sleep to make it into work on time.

What I didn't know was my life would be a tough one again and this time was worse than the last time. All of it was bad but I think this one would be the worst of all. Being drugged by two people was bad enough but nothing like what was coming to me. I think that I would have felt better if I would have died by suicide. I know that was a horrible thing to say and I am glad that my feelings have changed now in my life.

Sometimes there is only enough that one person can take of the trauma in their lives but I've learned that if I just hold on long enough, things will get better in time.

CHAPTER

12

I began to really get involved in the security ministry I was serving in. I would go to church all three services on Sundays and drove a security cart most of the time. I really loved the ministry and there were a lot of nice and friendly people at the church. I met an Usher who was really nice and he prayed for me a lot of the time. I was grateful for his prayers and defiantly needed his prayers in months to follow.

I moved into a studio room in Garden Grove from a girl I met at work. I loved my new room and for once, I was alone. I fixed the room up and had a bed finally that I liked to lay on in the summer months with a fan blowing on me while I watched television. It was great.

I remember laying in bed on night and I felt a hit and then my body jerked like I had been shocked. I jumped and wondered what it was that just happened to me. After laying in bed a little longer, the same thing happened to me again. I didn't know what was going on but I was being hit by something. They were really hard hits and I finally went to my truck to try and sleep some.

I kept getting hit in my truck so I went back to my room to lay down in my bed. I wondered if it was my illness and thought my body was just jumping from nerve endings in my back and legs. As the night went on the hits got harder and harder. Later I began to get hit and shocked at the same time. I was horrible!

The next day I told a friend in the security ministry and he said that I needed to see my doctor. He believed that it was my mental illness. I told him that I wasn't sick and that these were real hits and that they were very hard hits. I told him I wasn't sick and I haven't been in quit sometime. I asked for prayer and everyone thought I was crazy except one of the guys. I knew I was getting hit hard by something and I then hated to go home to try and sleep but I had to because I had to work on Sunday night.

I got hit hard a few times while sleeping but I was able to make it into work. At work I tried in my mind to figure out what was going on and I decided I would try and get my mind off of the situation that was happening to me.

The next night, Monday night I was off work and wanted to enjoy my night. I turned on some television and decided to go and get something to eat. When I got back at home I decided I would try and sleep some. I finally dozed off to sleep. I started getting hit again really hard in my legs and my back. I would jump in pain. I again went to my truck to try and sleep and I kept getting jerked and hit. Again, I decided to go back to my room.

When I got back to my room, I took a lot of my medication to be able to sleep during the hits. After a while, the beatings stopped and I was able to sleep. This went on for about three months and then the beatings got a lot worse. What ever it was that was beating me began to shake my bed and bang on the walls.

I figured that because I was getting hit in my truck and other places that there was no need in moving out of the house because it would happed wherever I went to. Because I could hear the walls being banged on and whatever it was walking around in my room, I began wearing ear plugs to bed. In-between hits I would be able to sleep about three minutes at a time. I would get to bed early in the afternoon so my minutes of sleep would add up to about two or three hours of sleep. I had to sleep, I worked at night. I did what worked and didn't know what to do about it. I asked God to help in prayer but that didn't work either.

One day when I got home from serving on the security team, I was laying in bed and just when I dozed off, whatever it was picked my head up and slammed it into the mattress. It was a hard slam and I got a head ackee. I knew without a doubt that I was being attacked by demons. It was an ongoing fight and anywhere that I tried to sleep at, I was under attack and kept getting hit really hard.

I tried sleeping in hotels and would get hit there. I went to visit my sister in South Carolina and got beat really bad there too. The demons would not leave me alone and I thought that the only way out of the attacks was suicide. I wasn't going to do that because God had brought me through so much in my life. I decided to find a way to live under attack.

I remember that every day that I would drive home from work, I would tell God that it was time for my beating. Finally, I decided that I would put the book of Psalms on my phone headset and fall asleep praying the Psalms in my head as I would hear the Psalms playing. I eventually was able to sleep during the beatings and the Bible, book of Psalms, made it possible.

I was more into praying then I was acknowledging the beatings. It worked for about three years. Every day I would do this and I was able to sleep but at times the beatings were so severe that I would wake up once in a while.

One afternoon while I was laying in bed, my little trash can that was on the floor by my desk, it went flying across the room. I just shook my head, got up and put the trash can back where it belonged. I began talking to the demons and this made them really mad.

On the following weekend as I was sleeping, I was grabbed from behind and chocked. The demon then grabbed my head and began to slam my head into the mattress. I decided that this apparently was their home and I had to move out immediately. I began to look for a place and I found a studio apartment in Buena Park, California.

I made an appointment and I didn't care how much it cost. This time I was living on my own, alone. I gave a deposit and paid the first months rent and moved in right away. I didn't waste anymore time. I was out of that house and was hoping that the problem with the attacks would stop.

The day I left, that night I got a whole pint of bourbon alcohol and drank the whole bottle. I waited to see if anything would happen to me. I was chocked a few times but I only got attacked by demons maybe twice a month now. It's somewhat tolerable now.

I am now living in my studio apartment in Buena Park and I love it here. I don't know how I survived the beatings but I did and the trauma I now feel, I don't know how I made it through. I did make it through and I will never forget these beatings. God is faithful though and I am making it now. Thank God for that!

After I moved into my apartment in Buena Park, I wanted to get a kitty cat. I was really lonely and wanted a companion so I looked up adoptions for animals at a Pet-Co store. Pet-Co is an animal pet store. I found an adoption agency through the store and they said on a Saturday they had kitties to adopt in cages outside of the store. On a Saturday I went and bought a litter box and some litter and cat food.

I then went to Pet-Co and looked at the cats. I saw a female tabby cat that was one-year-old and I liked her. I decided to get her so they put her in a box and I took her home with me. At first, she was really scared a would hide under my bed. After about two weeks, she finally came out from under the bed and let me pet her. She is the sweetest kitty I had ever had. I love her so much.

I decided to adopt another kitty and this time I adopted a male; black Siamese and he is so wonderful to have. He doesn't like to be held but he always wants to be pet while I'm in bed. These two cats are my only family out here and I don't know what I would do without them. They have really helped my emotions during some really severe depression.

My female tabby's name is Muffin and my male, black kitty is named Seth. I have had some hard days, and knowing that I would be coming home after work to be with them has, for me, made all the difference in how I feel.

There was a time that I was so depressed, I wanted to die. I told a friend of mine at work that I wanted to go to a gun store, buy a gun, and shoot myself in the parking lot sitting in my truck. The only thought that I had was, who will take care of my kitties? I decided that I didn't want them to go to a shelter so my thoughts and feelings changed.

These cats are like my children I never had. I love them very much and want to see to that they feel loved at all times. I spend a lot on them but their worth it to me. They are very special and I think to myself when I'm around them that maybe I will make it at last.

I began praying and asking God to take the depression away. I decided that I didn't want to live in depression anymore, so I understand that I have to give my life entirely to Christ and let him help me. So far, he has. He is very faithful and trust worthy and I know that I will be okay in his hands.

There is a little Church that a friend of mine from work told me about on Knot Avenue near where I live and I am going to be attending services there. As far as the security team at my other church that I attended, I stepped down from ministry there. I had moved and the drive was too far to continue serving there. Also, the man that is now in charge of the security ministry only wants men on the team. That's okay with me. I wonder what they are going to do if they ever need to deal with a female church goer.

A friend of mine sent a message to me on my phone, Jeramiah 29:11 and it says

"For I know the thoughts that I think toward you, says the Lord, thoughts of peace and not of evil, to give you a future and a hope."

When I got that scripture, it changed my life and my outlook on everything. I think to myself, maybe there is some hope and that I might one day be able to help those people who have been through hard trauma and trials. I always wanted to be a trauma counselor in a church somewhere. I will just have to wait and see what God does in my life.

I feel the future for me is bright and now I look forward to waking up from sleep every day. I thank God for his grace and mercy in my life.

I would like to say to whomever may read my words that there is real hope in God. I made it so can you. There is a way that God only knows that can restore a person and their lives. I've learned that if I don't give up hope and just hold on a little while longer, things always get better. I believe that things will get better for my reader too. Remember, never give up!